The
Political Economy
of the Cotton South

The
Political Economy
of the Cotton South

Households, Markets, and
Wealth in the
Nineteenth Century

GAVIN WRIGHT

UNIVERSITY OF MICHIGAN

W · W · NORTON & COMPANY · INC ·
NEW YORK

Copyright © 1978 by W. W. Norton & Company, Inc. Published
simultaneously in Canada by George J. McLeod Limited, Toronto.
Printed in the United States of America.

ALL RIGHTS RESERVED

FIRST EDITION

Library of Congress Cataloging in Publication Data
Wright, Gavin.
    The political economy of the cotton South.
    Bibliography: p.
    Includes index.
    1. Southern States—Economic conditions.
2. Cotton trade—Southern States—History.
I. Title.
HC107.A13W68   330.9'75'04   77-26715
ISBN 0-393-05686-4
ISBN 0-393-09038-8 pbk.

1 2 3 4 5 6 7 8 9 0

For my parents,
Charles F. Wright and
Agnita Greisen Wright

Contents

TABLES, FIGURES, AND MAPS

Tables

Figures

Maps

Preface

The American South has largely severed its ties to cotton during its twentieth-century economic and political resurgence, but neither the region nor the nation has yet escaped from the influence of an earlier era of regional prominence dominated by King Cotton. Much of Southern economic history in recent decades has been an undoing of the patterns of demographic location and economic activity that emerged in the nineteenth century and persisted into the twentieth. Even as Southern homogeneity and distinctiveness have faded, however, it remains true that the least affluent Americans are disproportionately Southerners, former Southerners, and their children, black and white. If the South was the nation's number one economic problem in the 1930s, as Roosevelt said, then the nation's quite different economic problems of the 1970s continue to have a Southern tinge. For these reasons it is worth our while to try to understand the historical background, the origins of the economic structure and institutions of the Cotton South, and the ways in which they evolved and changed over the course of the nineteenth century.

The chapters that follow represent the culmination of an intellectual odyssey that has spanned more than a decade. My interest in the Southern economy goes back to my experience in the civil rights movement of the early 1960s. I was eager to accept the opportunity to return to North Carolina in the summer of 1966 as a research assistant on a project directed by Professors Robert Gallman of the University of North Carolina and William N. Parker, my teacher at Yale. The central purpose of that study was to measure the degree of self-sufficiency of the antebellum cotton economy, as a test of Douglass North's hypothesis which stressed the importance of inter-regional trade flows in early American development. Since then, several studies have confirmed the Parker-Gallman conclusion that the extent of self-sufficiency in basic foodstuffs was quite high. But it was only some time later that I came to realize, along with Gallman, that self-sufficiency was not just a matter of the aggregate balance in regional trade flows, but was a basic behavioral feature of Southern farming in the antebellum era.

At Parker's request, my first investigation concerned the issue of economies of scale under slavery. At that time I believed that if one were to find no positive economies of scale, one could support an interpretation of planter behavior based on cultural, psychological, or other noneconomic motives. It was several years before I concluded that in the real world of uncertainty, the attempt to distinguish "economic" from "noneconomic" motives was hopeless. And it was some years more before I came to see, with Heywood Fleisig's help, that the key to understanding the connection between slavery and scale was to understand the barriers to expansion faced by free family farms. The distinctive character of the family farm had been a central theme of Parker's lectures and writing for some time, but, slow learner that I was, I did not see the connection until after I had left Yale.

There was a third intellectual thread of more or less independent origins: the attempt to apply econometric methods to the cotton economy as a whole in the context of worldwide demand and competing supplies. This work began with a term paper for Marc Nerlove's econometrics course at Yale; with Nerlove's encouragement, the research continued and the paper was ultimately published. It took ten years for me to realize that these three strands could be woven into a coherent interpretation of the course of the Southern economy over the nineteenth century as a whole.

As I have had to revise my original conceptions on many of these points, so too my thinking has changed about the relationship between history and economics. These early years were the heyday of the New Economic History, the self-conscious application of economic analysis and econometric techniques to historical subjects. The fruits of this movement have frequently been valuable and stimulating, but I now believe that it is a mistake for economic history to define itself merely as economics applied to old data. Instead, economic history offers a distinctive intellectual approach to the study of economics, a view of the economic world in which historical time plays a fundamental role. Resource allocation is affected not just by the interaction of tastes and technology at time t, but also by the experience and endowment of the past. Initial conditions do matter, and the historical order of events does matter; a given stimulus may evoke radically different responses at different historical times. Nonetheless, the reader should be warned that this remains an economist's history, in that it stresses analysis and strives for an economy of explanation, fitting the evidence into the simplest logical framework needed to make the argument. There is no claim here that all relevant aspects of the cotton economy have been covered.

Several individuals have been particularly important in the development of the book. I have drawn heavily on the insights and suggestions of Heywood Fleisig. Certain sections of chapter 3 could well bear his name rather than mine, though he is not responsible for the use I have made of his ideas. In two other cases I have made use of previous work that was jointly authored: chapter 5 makes use of an article on slave prices and territorial expansion that was coauthored by Peter Passell; and the discussion of crop choice in chapters 3 and 6 relies on my research with Howard Kunreuther. In writing chapter 2, I have benefited from an excellent term paper on cotton and soil exhaustion written by Algis Glamba, a graduate student in history at Michigan.

I am also grateful to Robert Fogel and Stanley Engerman, whose own work on slavery has been highly influential. The academic year 1970–71, which I spent on leave at the University of Chicago, was a time of great excitement and stimulation during the writing of their book *Time on the Cross*. At that time my research concerned other matters and my ideas on the Southern economy were poorly formed.

It was only when I began work on a critique of their book two years later that the synthesis that appears here began to emerge. If our interpretations continue to differ, readers should know that the chapters below do not fairly indicate how much I owe to discussions and correspondence with each of these men over many years' time.

My colleagues at the University of Michigan have been generous with valuable advice and criticism, especially Gary Saxonhouse, Ronald Lee, Richard Porter, Saul Hymans, Harold Shapiro, and historians Jacob Price and Mills Thornton. Among the many others from whom I have received suggestions or with whom I have had helpful discussions, I would like to thank Paul David, Richard Sutch, Roger Ransom, Joseph D. Reid, Jr., Robert Higgs, Albert Fishlow, Phil Mirowski, Jay Mandle, Eugene Genovese, Alan Olmstead, Stephen DeCanio, Peter Temin, Ralph V. Anderson, Jan de Vries, Claudia Goldin, Mark Schmitz and Don Schaefer. Earlier discussions with Daniel Crofts and Paul Worthman have been more influential than either of them probably realizes. My first interest in economics is mainly traceable to Joseph Conard's seminar at Swarthmore College; this would be a better book if it did not suffer from the untimely loss of his counsel and advice.

The study uses the Parker-Gallman sample from the 1860 Cotton South and a smaller 1850 sample collected by James D. Foust. I have also made some use of the Batemen-Foust sample of Northern households in 1860; I thank Fred Bateman and James Foust for permission to use the data, and Jeremy Atack for his assistance in using it. All of these samples were obtained with the financial assistance of the National Science Foundation. Research support for some of the background work was provided by the Rackham School at the University of Michigan. The actual drafting of the manuscript was made possible by a fellowship from the John Simon Guggenheim Foundation. Robert Kehoe of W. W. Norton & Company improved the manuscript markedly with an unusually conscientious job of editing.

My wife, Cathe, suggested that the book should be called

"Soil, Toil and Moil." That must often have seemed the right name for her part in our family enterprise of raising two vigorous boys while continuing our separate pursuits in economic history and in theatre. Through it all, however, I have been sustained and enriched by the love and fellowship of my family.

G.W.

The
Political Economy
of the Cotton South

1

Introduction

This book attempts to show how observed patterns of resource allocation, production, and economic change in the
American South may be understood in terms of a few basic
principles, which reflect the internal logic of various economic situations and institutions. It goes somewhat beyond
economic history narrowly defined into questions of class
relationships and political behavior. Though an exercise in
"econometric history," this work is not based on vast moun-
tains of new data, it contains little mathematics, and it
uses only relatively simple statistical techniques. This is also
a book about slavery, but it does not explore the slave per-
sonality, the slave family, nor the slave community, and it
does not try to penetrate the subtleties and ambiguities of
the master-slave relationship. Rather than define significant
new historical questions, it addresses the old standbys of
Southern history: the profitability of slavery before the Civil
War, the overproduction of cotton after the Civil War, the
effects of slavery on regional progress, and the causes of the
war. A book of such modest scope has to justify itself on two
fronts: its relationship to previous economic analyses of slavery and of the nineteenth-century Southern economy, and its
relationship to the larger body of historical literature on slavery and the South.

Models, Economists, and Slavery

A major flourishing of historical economic analysis of slavery dates from the 1958 Conrad and Meyer study on the profitability of slavery.[1] The distinguishing feature of this work has been the application of basic economic principles of competitive market economies (principles commonly referred to as "price theory") to the analysis of slavery. Generally, economists have found the slave economy readily amenable to their approach; its main features are well explained by price theory, and slavery seems to have functioned flexibly and efficiently in response to economic incentives, even generating a rapid rate of economic progress until the Civil War.[2] The justification for another contribution to this stream is that this book advocates a new approach, a new set of behavioral assumptions, and a new set of benchmarks for comparison—in each case, "new" in relation to the economic literature, but rooted more firmly in the historical setting and in contemporary characterizations.

There is some tendency for historians to take a "bottom line" approach to the economic literature, concluding, for example, that because almost all the economists agree that slavery was profitable, there is little reason for the layman to try to master the fine points of the debate. This kind of reading is not safe, because the "profitability" which Conrad and Meyer support is of a particular kind, having to do with the appropriateness of slave prices in relationship to returns. This is very different from the kind of profitability analyzed by Yasuba, which has to do with the more fundamental

1. "The Economics of Slavery in the Antebellum South," reprinted in *The Economics of Slavery and Other Studies in Econometric History,* eds., Alfred H. Conrad and John R. Meyer (Chicago: Aldine, 1964). Many of the subsequent contributions are collected in Hugh Aitken, ed., *Did Slavery Pay?*

2. In addition to those in the previous footnote, the most important citations are Robert Fogel and Stanley Engerman, *Time on the Cross* and Claudia Goldin, *Urban Slavery in the American South 1820–1860.* On regional progress, the favorable assessment of slavery's contribution is summarized most recently by Stanley Engerman, "A Reconsideration of Southern Economic Growth, 1770–1860."

relationship between returns and the cost of reproducing the slave labor force.[3] Historical interpretations based on one concept may be completely irrelevant to the other. This is only one example of the need for a close look at the underlying specification of a question and the underlying assumptions of an analysis.

Some of the important assumptions of conventional economic analysis, basic to most of the existing research in econometric history, are as follows:

(1) that profit maximization is a reasonable approximation to the principle governing the behavior of firms and farms in history

(2) that the relative scarcities of basic factors of production, such as land and labor, are reflected in their relative prices

(3) that the principle of opportunity costs implies that there is no essential difference between the production and consumption of nonmarket goods and services on the one hand, and the production, sale and purchase of commodities through the market, except for the costs of transportation and other costs directly associated with transactions

(4) that regional progress is best measured by the rate of growth of regional income per capita, and that this progress may be partitioned into growth in factor inputs and increases in the productivity of these inputs

(5) that "economic" interpretations of political behavior have to do with actual or potential effects on the real incomes of participants.

Not every economist is committed to every one of these assumptions, and no one has proclaimed that these are eternal truths for all of history; but these are the working presuppositions that economists typically bring to the subject. Anyone can see that these are simplifying operational assumptions, and any analytical history of manageable proportions is bound to involve a rather drastically simplified

3. Yasukichi Yasuba, "The Profitability and Viability of Plantation Slavery in the United States."

characterization of behavior and the workings of markets. My objection to writing a history constrained by these assumptions is not that they are too simple, but that they are fundamentally inappropriate to antebellum America, where most farmers were family farmowners whose most critical decisions involved the choice between market and nonmarket economic activity, and who had reason to be as concerned with wealth as with real income. The models developed in this book are also simple, but they place these historical elements at the center of the analysis. And as it happens, a modest adaptation to historical circumstances produces an analysis that supports such "traditional" propositions as the following: that slavery retarded the mechanization of agriculture, the development of manufacturing, the emergence of cities, and immigration into the South; that the South was on the verge of economic crisis in 1860; that tenancy and associated credit systems caused "overproduction" of cotton after the war; and that the Civil War was fundamentally caused by the economics of slavery. These assertions do not sound original, but surely it is worth something to show that they can be derived from simple models of economic behavior and supported with econometric evidence.

As the foregoing suggests, many of the criticisms leveled at recent work on the economics of slavery will apply to this book as well: for example, the use of aggregate data to analyze a heterogeneous region; the reliance on evidence from the late antebellum period in the study of a slave system which evolved over more than two centuries; and the failure to treat the slaves themselves as independent psychological agents, at least not until they emerge as tenant farmers after the war. There is some justice in all these complaints. But limits of data are not as constricting as limits of vision, and there is a reason and purpose for the strategy of the book. While the geographical diversity of the South is acknowledged and incorporated at many points, the chapters which follow argue that it was in the nature of cotton and slavery during this era to impose an organic economic unity on the region as a whole, most notably through the common interest in the value of slave property. Trends in the distribution of wealth and in the class structure of Southern society are appropriately studied at an aggregate level, because high rates of migration frequently make the evidence from smaller geographic units misleading. On the representativeness of the time period, the treatment here tries to make up for limits of data by explicitly placing the late antebellum decades in the historical context of an unprecedented growth of demand for an industrial raw material, of which the American South was the world's dominant supplier. Lack of perspective on slavery derives not just from ignoring the eighteenth century background but from ignoring what came *after* 1860, the failure to see the coherence of Southern economic history over the nineteenth century as a whole.[4]

The neglect of slave behavior and slave-management behavior requires more comment. These are not unimportant aspects of history, either for the history of slavery or for the post-slave history of Afro-Americans and the South. The recent attention to the attitudes, personalities, families, and communities of slaves is altogether healthy.[5] But slavery also occupies an essentially logical place in the evolution of American agricultural systems and property rights, and the way to understand this logical place is not to apply a microscope to either the planter or the slave, but to examine the behavior of free farmers, North and South. Master-slave relationships must surely be important in explaining variations in productivity among farms and plantations, but there is little evidence of a genuine difference in physical productivity between typical free farmers and typical slaves, nor of genuine productivity gains over time under slavery. In-

---

4. Roger Ransom and Richard Sutch, in their book on the post-bellum South, *One Kind of Freedom*, similarly find that a close backward look at slavery is essential to a study of the later period.

5. In addition to Fogel and Engerman, the most prominent citations are John Blassingame, *The Slave Community*; Eugene D. Genovese, *Roll, Jordan, Roll*; Herbert Gutman, *The Black Family in Slavery and Freedom, 1750–1925*; and Leslie Howard Owens, *This Species of Property*.

stead, the economic essence of slavery involved the ability
of the owner to control the allocation of labor time between market and nonmarket activity.

The book is addressed to historians, economic historians,
historical economists, and the students of all three. Each of
these groups may take particular interest in one or another
part of the book, but the analysis forms an integrated whole.
Some sections are unavoidably technical, but throughout
the book an effort has been made to keep the material ac-
cessible to all readers, and the central themes are not really
difficult. Indeed, some historians will undoubtedly say that
some parts of the argument are really obvious after all, an
allegation which, if true, is a severe indictment of the economics profession. But even when arguments seem obvious
in retrospect, there is a virtue in being formal and systematic, because there is also much that is confused and inconsistent in the historical literature, and the approach has led
to many further inferences that were not at all obvious at
the outset. Virtually all readers will find parts of the argument neither obvious nor traditional.

Finally, it should be clear that the book is not an attack
on or rebuttal to any other works of scholarship, but an
independent effort to develop an integrated interpretation.
It does not carry on a debate with Robert W. Fogel and
Stanley Engerman's *Time on the Cross,* a book that delves
into many topics not touched on here. The book does owe
a great deal to the work of these two scholars, and to discussions and correspondence with them over several years,
even if in the end its point of view is different. Some
readers will feel that some of the same things are expressed
here in a different way. This is true enough, but "how you
say it" is much of what matters on the interface between
economics and history.

The Argument Summarized

A brief outline may help to guide the reader. Chapter 2
sketches the historical background to the antebellum era

and then describes the geographical patterns of cotton-growing, slaveholding, and wealth as they stood in 1860. Several problems are posed for subsequent chapters. How is it that median farm size is not much different North and South, but average farm size and the concentration of farm wealth are substantially greater in the South; and yet the overall concentration of wealth in the North seems roughly similar to that in the South? How is it that the farm-by-farm association between cotton and slavery is so close, yet the aggregate distribution of slaveholdings seems to date back before the cotton era and to be remarkably stable over time? Even during the 1850s, the degree of inequality in Southern wealthholding was not notably increasing in the aggregate, despite a great deal of geographic reshuffling of farmers and planters; what is the significance, then, of the growing divergence in wealth between slaveholders in the South and nonslaveholders everywhere?

An explanation for these facts is set out in chapter 3, with a simple model in which the character of labor supply is the main constraint on the expansion of individual farms in the early nineteenth century. Slave plantations are seen as family farms for which this constraint has been relaxed, allowing an expansion in scale which family farms in the free states could not achieve. Within the South, the primary difference between plantations and farms is not in the efficiency of production but in the choice of outputs, specifically the division between marketed and nonmarketed production. Under slavery, "labor was a commodity" and its allocation is well explained by the principles of price theory; but this was not so for family labor on smaller farms, where immediate risks and long-range objectives dictated a more limited production for the market.

The implications of these alternative economic structures for regional growth and development are explored in chapter 4. Fluctuations in the South's rate of economic growth during the nineteenth century are not the responsibility of Southern institutions, but are explained by trends in world cotton demand. Even the devastation of the Civil

War was no more damaging to the regional economy than the end of the long cotton boom of the antebellum period. The South's specialization in agriculture is satisfactorily explained by the principle of comparative advantage, but this is precisely what was wrong, not right, with the regional economy. Under slavery, the South lacked the creative tensions which generated a manufacturing sector in the North: specifically, the impulse to mechanization in agriculture; the development of an industrial labor force; the funneling of entrepreneurial talent into manufacturing; and the promotion of cities, towns, and internal improvements by landowners.

Regional differences in property ownership and in the determination of property values had political consequences as well, which are treated in chapter 5. Whereas the concern for land values led Northerners to devote their energies to transportation, immigration, town building, and the politics of local and territorial development, the pre-eminence of slave values focused the attention of Southerners on national politics and matters of high principle. The political behavior of slaveowners is understandable as an effort to maintain the value of slave property at levels well above the costs of replacement—hence at levels particularly sensitive to changes in expectations and to political threats, real or potential. As befits the topic, chapter 5 is somewhat more speculative and venturesome than the rest, but the argument flows naturally from the analysis and evidence presented earlier.

Chapter 6 takes the story to the end of the century, arguing that the economic problems of the South had less to do with the war, Reconstruction, and the immediate legacy of slavery than with stagnation in world cotton demand. These problems were aggravated, however, by the historical coincidence of high cotton prices, wartime destruction, and the rise of tenancy—developments that combined to push the region more deeply than ever into cotton at the very time when it should have moved away. Thus the failure to develop a diversified nonagricultural sector under slavery had serious costs. At the same time, the struggles and frustrations of tenants and indebted farmers after the war offer a vivid illustration of the fears which led free farmers to limit their involvement with the market, when they had the choice. On these grounds, close attention to the postwar behavior and experience is essential to understanding slavery and the antebellum South.

2

The Structure of the
Cotton-Slave Economy

What was the economic basis for plantation slavery, and how did slavery affect the structure of Southern society? In order to answer questions like these, we need a clearer picture of the empirical outlines of the cotton-slave economy. Was the slave plantation typical or exceptional in the Cotton South? Were typical slaves on large or small units? Were output and wealth becoming increasingly concentrated in the hands of large slaveowners? All of these seem to be straightforward, objective questions, yet historians have continued to answer them in divergent ways, notwithstanding the fact that the basic sources of information have not changed in over a century. The persistence of these differing interpretations does not mainly reflect poor data or inadequate statistical techniques. Instead, the "planter dominance" and "economic democracy" hypotheses still find advocates, for the good reason that each one reflects real features of antebellum Southern society. The elaboration of this paradox is the main business of this chapter.

The Rise of Cotton and North American Slavery

The elementary economic logic of slavery in a setting of land abundance has been outlined many times: [1] if land is available to all comers, and if cultivation may be practiced at any scale without major loss of efficiency, then there will be no way for an entrepreneur to achieve a large absolute profit except with unfree labor. Under a free labor system, wages would rise to exhaust all land rents. For some time, the system of indentured servitude functioned effectively in this situation, as workers contracted to repay their transportation costs from Europe with a term of service. Most of the seventeenth-century development of tobacco culture in Virginia and Maryland was based on white indentured labor, in a system with many of the economic features of slavery—men and women could be bought and sold at any time, families broken up, harsh punishments inflicted for running away or misbehavior, and some planters were able to expand their operations well beyond family scale. Indentured servitude was inherently transitional, however: as terms of service were completed, as free-labor wages rose and the cost of transport fell, only the full-fledged system of involuntary slavery-for-life survived.[2]

Land-labor conditions were initially similar in all of the colonies, as were attitudes toward profit-making and slavery. What is missing from this story is the fact that in the seventeenth and eighteenth centuries, North American colonies had to buy African slaves on a world market at prices which reflected the high profitability of slavery in the sugar colonies of the West Indies. For this reason, despite the underlying similarity in factor proportions, slavery expanded only in areas where profitable export staples were available. Though cotton was of no commercial importance before the 1780s, the growth of North American slavery revolved pri-

1. Most recently, Evsey Domar, "The Causes of Slavery or Serfdom: A Hypothesis."
2. See Edmund S. Morgan, *American Slavery, American Freedom*, especially chapters 6–7, 11–12.

marily around the fortunes of tobacco and rice, with indigo playing a briefer and lesser part in the mid-eighteenth century. In the North, according to a leading student of anti-slavery thought, "the original and essential grievance of the colonists who cared about the matter was that they could not buy enough slaves at a reasonable price." [3]

Some authorities have attempted to explain the geographic concentration of slavery on the basis of general aspects of the Southern environment, such as climate, soils, diseases, and the length of the growing season. [4] But the number of crops involved is so few that there is little point in constructing an abstract theory to account for their availability: the important point is that they were only found in the South. There was no inherent incompatability between slavery and Northern climes and crops; it was strictly a matter of relative returns. The geographic distribution of the free population was determined by a host of social, cultural, legal, and psychological, as well as economic, considerations, but as a general rule, slave labor followed the market. This market-determined difference of the eighteenth century became a legal and political distinction in the nineteenth century, as the Northern states all moved toward full abolition of slavery by the 1790s. [5] In one sense, Northern abolition was no more than a legal ratification of the regional separation that economic opportunities had originally brought about. But if this legal step had not been taken, the increasing profitability of Northern grain crops might well have allowed the spread of slavery into the Northwest territory in the nineteenth century. Despite the proscription of slavery in the Northwest Ordinances of the 1780s, strong proslavery forces continued to struggle for legalization in Indiana until 1809 and in Illinois into the 1820s. The Illi-

3. David Brion Davis, *The Problem of Slavery in Western Culture*, p. 135. Davis's quotation is directed at all the colonies, but he clearly intends to include the North (pp. 125, 135–36).

4. For example, F. V. Emerson, "Geographic Influences in American Slavery."

5. New York and New Jersey were laggard. See Arthur Zilversmit, *The First Emancipation*.

nois territory, which was separated from Indiana over the slavery issue, had a proslavery majority as late as 1818. Only the threat of congressional rejection deterred Illinois from attempting to enter the Union as a slave state.[6] Thus, nineteenth-century history down to 1860 offers a case study of comparative regional development under alternative institutional systems, in which the legal regime was the effective obstacle to slavery in the North.

In the South, slavery was never in serious danger, but what doubts there were dissipated with the appearance of cotton in the South in the 1790s. The significance of the rise of cotton in the 1790s was that it opened up a much broader area of the South to commercial agriculture and the profitable use of slaves. The emergence of cotton is typically dated from Whitney's invention of the cotton gin in 1793, but it now seems clear that the appearance of the gin was only a dramatic episode in a process which had its origins in demand-side pressure. The high profitability of sea-island cotton during 1785–95 stimulated many attempts to grow this long-staple variety farther inland; however, only the short-staple green-seed cotton would grow in the upland areas. This development, in turn, created the bottleneck that called forth Whitney's gin, because the fuzzy fibers of upland cotton clung to the seeds and could not be separated with the old roller gin. In the year preceding Whitney's arrival in Georgia, it is estimated that two to three million pounds of short-staple had been harvested, only a small fraction of which had been ultimately cleaned and sold.[7] The state of Georgia had appointed a commission to promote the invention of a suitable gin, and the great concern

6. Theodore Calvin Pease, *The Story of Illinois* (Chicago: University of Chicago Press, 1949), pp. 72–80; William W. Freehling, "The Founding Fathers and Slavery," p. 87. See also John. D. Bernhart, *Valley of Democracy: The Frontier vs. the Plantation in the Ohio Valley, 1775–1818* (Lincoln: University of Nebraska Press, 1970; originally published 1953), chaps. 9–13.

7. Matthew B. Hammond, *The Cotton Industry*, p. 23; Lewis C. Gray, *History of Agriculture in the Southern United States to 1860*, pp. 678–83.

and discussion over the matter is what captured Whitney's interest. As Nevins and Mirsky summarize: "Never did an American invention meet a more urgent need than Whitney's. . . . Its appearance could have been predicted with reasonable accuracy; the gin to clean green-seed cotton could not have been delayed long after." [8] The prime mover in the rise of the Cotton Kingdom was thus the Industrial Revolution itself, and from this date forward the fortunes of the Southern economy were closely tied to the progress of the British textile industry.

On the supply side, the rise of cotton and slavery turned on two decisive geo-economic facts, which appear contradictory but which are nonetheless both true: first, cotton could be successfully cultivated with varying yields in almost all sections of the South below 37° north latitude; second, the particular combination of soils, temperature patterns, rainfall, and growing season found in the cotton belt was uniquely suited for production of the varieties of cotton most in demand during the nineteenth century. The first of these meant that cotton allowed slavery to escape its narrow geographical enclaves on the coast. But cotton could also be grown by small-scale free farmers; nonperishability and high value in relation to weight made it commercially feasible quite far inland—onto the Appalachian Piedmont, the lower Mississippi Valley, and even the interior of Alabama, Mississippi, and Tennessee.[9] For most of the South, cotton was the only crop with these characteristics in the nineteenth century. But while cotton, once picked, is sturdy and durable, the cotton plant is extremely sensitive to characteristics of climate. It requires a minimum of 200 to 210 frostless days and twenty to twenty-five inches of rainfall. However, the need for water varies according to the time of season: heavy rains in the early spring will limit the depth of the root system; rains at harvesttime will cause the fruit to fall off and

8. Jeanette Mirsky and Allan Nevins, *The World of Eli Whitney* (New York: Macmillan Co., 1952), p. 81.
9. Gray, pp. 683–89; Carroll P. Wilsie, *Crop Adaptation and Distribution* (San Francisco: W. H. Freeman & Co., 1962), p. 373.

interfere with picking. In the American Cotton Belt, rainfall tends to increase from spring to midsummer and then progressively to decrease, approaching an ideal pattern.[10] Modern irrigation technology can reproduce these patterns artificially, but in the nineteenth century the South was unmatched. Furthermore, the distinctive American upland variety had a qualitative superiority to all others available; it could not be matched for "uniting strength of fibre with smoothness and length of staple." [11] These geographic conditions are the basic unifying threads for the economic history of the South in the nineteenth and much of the twentieth century. From the 1790s the United States became the world's dominant supplier within a generation, exerting a determining influence on the world price. Cotton gave the South a prosperity, growth, and unity that it could not otherwise have had. But, the very uniqueness of the crop rendered it a weakness as well as a strength, the more so in the long run because of its close attachment to slavery.

The Cotton South in 1860

The western expansion of the cotton belt proceeded with remarkable speed and persistence down to the Civil War. The pace was not altogether uniform, the major deviations from the trend coming with the demand-initiated boom of the 1830s and the subsequent slump of the early 1840s. But on the whole, antebellum cotton demand was ebullient, and migration continued even in slack times. Typically, small slaveless farmers were the first to move, but the movement of the slave population into the richest cotton areas of the Southwest was also rapid. The strong momentum is largely explained by the natural superiority of cotton land in the

10. Harry Bates Brown, *Cotton*, pp. 97, 229–30; Wilsie, p 369; Milton Whitney, "Climatology and Soils," in *The Cotton Plant*, United States Office of Agricultural Experiment Stations Bulletin No. 33, pp. 144–45; James R. Covert, "Seedtime and Harvest," p. 93.
    11. C. F. McCay, "Cultivation of Cotton," pp. 117–18.

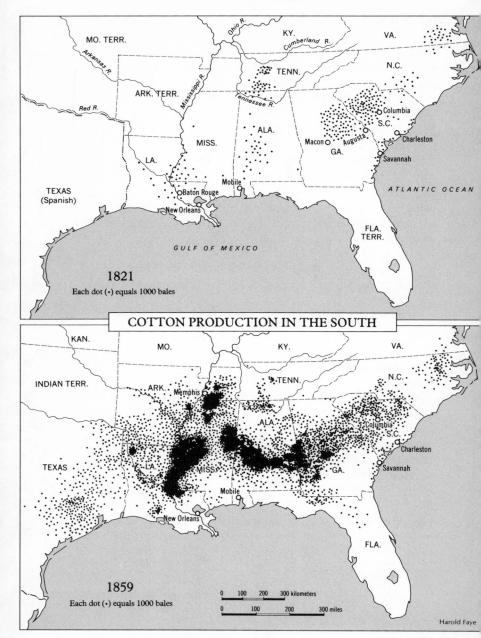

COTTON PRODUCTION IN THE SOUTH

1821
Each dot (•) equals 1000 bales

1859
Each dot (•) equals 1000 bales

0   100   200   300 kilometers
0   100   200   300 miles

Harold Faye

Adapted from United States Department of Agriculture, *Atlas of Agriculture*, Part V, Advance Sheets (December 15, 1915).

old Southwest. The non-Ricardian character of the process, from inferior to superior soil, has given rise to greatly exaggerated conceptions of the extent of soil exhaustion and erosion in the Southeast. Cotton is not in fact a highly exhaustive crop, and the gutted, windswept hills of the Piedmont, so vividly described by Olmsted and De Bow, were as much the result of abandonment as its cause.[12] The migration of cotton and slaves was not a mindless east-west movement from exhausted to virgin soils, but a rational process of geographical expansion and relocation which continued along similar lines well after the war.

By the mid-nineteenth century, the Cotton Kingdom stretched from the Carolinas to east Texas, from northwest Florida to central and western Tennessee, and was expanding rapidly into Arkansas and the Texas plain. Much of this chapter is based on a sample of 5,229 farms from the manuscript census of 1860, from the 413 counties producing at least one thousand bales of cotton in that year.[13] This group of "cotton counties" forms a nearly contiguous belt through the heart of the South. So nearly distinct were the staple regions of the South in 1860 that the sample universe, which contains counties producing 98 percent of the nation's cotton crop, excludes 96 percent of the rice crop, 98 percent

12. On the relatively small demands made by cotton upon the plant food of the soil in comparison with other crops, see J. B. McBryde and W. H. Beal, "Chemistry of Cotton," pp. 83–84, and H. C. White, "The Manuring of Cotton," pp. 169–71, both in *The Cotton Plant.* For more modern citations, see Roy L. Donahue, *Soils* (Englewood Cliffs, New Jersey: Prentice-Hall, 1965), pp. 192–3; W. H. Allaway, "Cropping Systems and Soil," in *Yearbook of Agriculture, 1957,* U.S. Department of Agriculture (Washington, D.C.: Government Printing Office, 1957), p. 387.

13. This sample, which will be referred to as the "Parker-Gallman sample," was collected under the supervision of Robert Gallman and William N. Parker, supported by the National Science Foundation. The most complete description of the sampling procedures and characteristics of the sample may be found in James D. Foust, "The Yeoman Farmer and Westward Expansion of U.S. Cotton Production." Briefer descriptions may be found in W. N. Parker, ed., *The Structure of the Cotton Economy of the Antebellum South,* particularly the articles by Foust and Swan, and Wright.

TABLE 2.1.
Regional Characteristics of the Cotton South, 1860

	COTTON YIELD CLAIMED ON FRESH LAND (LBS./ACRE)	SLAVES AS % OF POPULATION	% FARMS WITH: 0 SLAVES	% FARMS WITH: 0 COTTON	% OF COTTON SOUTH TOTAL FARMS	% OF COTTON SOUTH TOTAL COTTON
Piedmont	500–800	43.1	43.4	20.7	18.9	10.8
Sand Hills	300–500	45.7	53.1	26.6	2.8	2.0
Valley	800–1,000	31.8	67.2	34.4	6.0	3.0
Western Upland	500–1,000	38.1	60.8	24.2	18.3	12.8
Black Prairie	800–1,000	68.1	28.5	11.1	5.0	13.4
Brown Loam	1,000–1,200	54.5	40.7	20.4	6.8	10.8
Central Plain	400–700	52.2	43.8	23.0	16.4	15.2
Coastal Plain	400–600	47.8	54.6	34.9	5.1	3.5
Alluvial	1,500–2,000	67.0	36.4	28.4	4.4	17.0
Cotton South		48.0	50.6	28.0	100.0	100.0

sources: Claimed cotton yield is from U.S. Census Office, 10th Census, 1880, Vol. 5 (Washington: GPO, 1883), p. 4; slaves as % of population computed from county figures in U.S. Census Office, 8th Census, 1860, Vol. 2 (Washington: GPO, 1864); remainder from Parker-Gallman sample (see text).

of the tobacco crop, and 75 percent of the cane sugar production.

Despite the distinctness, the Cotton South was not at all homogeneous in many respects. Within the South, regions differed markedly in soils, fertility, numbers of slaves, and average farm size. A few of these contrasts are collected in Table 2.1 for the major soil type regions used in this study. A brief survey of these regions will convey a sense of the diverse cross section which comprised the Cotton South in 1860.[14]

The *Piedmont* of the Carolinas and Georgia (reaching into eastern Alabama) was the first area of rapid expansion of cotton and slavery. Upland cotton takes its name from the irregular terrain of granite and metamorphic rock in this region. Despite its primacy, the Piedmont was by no means the most fertile cotton land in the country, but its decline from the early nineteenth century was only in relative, not absolute, terms. The Piedmont contained roughly one-fifth of the cotton-county farms in 1860, but produced only one-tenth of the cotton.

Between the *Piedmont* and the coast, from North Carolina to Mississippi, lies a gently sloping plain, which we divide into the inner *Central Plain* (soil type 23 in the 1880 census) and outer *Coastal Plain* (soil type 24). These soils are mainly sands and sandy loams, generally of below-average fertility, with the *Coastal Plain* the poorer of the two. The fall line between Piedmont and plain is marked by a smaller *Sand Hills* region of still lower fertility.

Southwest of the Piedmont and above the Coastal Plain lies the *Black Prairie* region of central Alabama and Mississippi. These stiff black calcareous soils are extremely fertile. Population and production grew rapidly in the 1830s and

14. The soil-type regions are based primarily on the soil types of the *Tenth Census of the United States Vol. V*, U.S. Census Office, 10th Census, 1880, Vol. V (Washington: GPO, 1883). It is obviously artificial to assume, as we are forced to do, that soil-type regions are bounded by county lines. But for the most part the counties of each soil type lie in roughly contiguous belts or clusters, with only a few borderline cases.

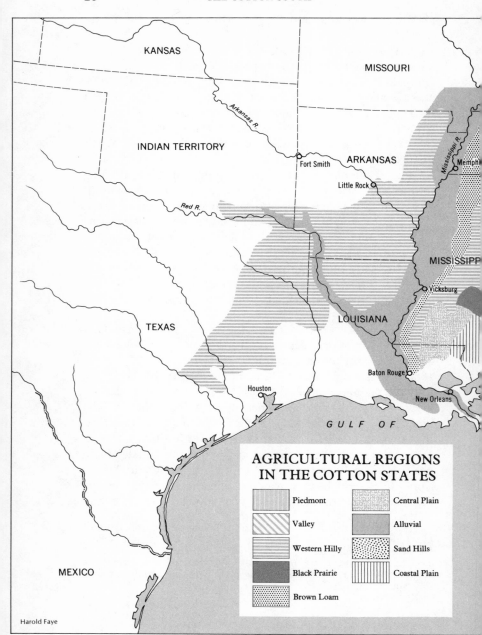

Adapted from U.S. Bureau of Census, U.S. Census of Population: 1880, Volume V.

1840s, and the region was second only to the alluvial low-
lands in cotton productivity and in the dominance of large
plantations. In northern Alabama and south central Tennessee lies another concentration of cotton and slaves, the
Valley lands of red calcareous soil along the Tennessee River.

The richest of the cotton regions were the *Alluvial* river
bottoms along the Mississippi in Louisiana, Mississippi, and
Arkansas, and along the Red River in Louisiana. This delta
region, in which we include three Texas counties at the
mouth of the Brazos, was easily the most naturally fertile in
the South. It contained the largest plantations and the highest concentration of slave population in 1860. East of the
delta in Mississippi and Tennessee lies the *Brown Loam*,
or "loess", region of mellow, siliceous loams. It is also fertile, but its soils are easily eroded, and it contained a much
more balanced mixture of farm sizes than the alluvium.
Both regions developed earlier than less fertile areas to the
east, but the alluvium was still rapidly expanding its cotton
output in the 1850s.

Above the delta on either side of the Mississippi is the
Western Upland region. Reaching from western Alabama
into east Texas, this so-called shortleaf pine hills region was
predominantly a small-farm area with relatively few concentrations of slaves. However, the soil of this region is as good
or better for cotton-growing than the Piedmont, and the
growth of population, cotton output, and slaves was rapid
in the 1850s. In Texas and Arkansas, this region contained
the western frontier of the Cotton South in the late antebellum period.

Historians have appropriately urged cliometricians to look
closely at regional distinctions such as these, and most of
the calculations in this book are done separately for each soil
type. Most obviously from Tables 2.1 and 2.2, any number
of statements about "typical" farm sizes and slaveholding
can be valid, depending on how much of the small-farm
regions on the periphery are included. The choices may be
extended further by including or excluding the rice and
sugar areas, and the tobacco, hemp, and general-farming
regions of the upper South. But while this diversity is ap-

TABLE 2.2.
DISTRIBUTION OF IMPROVED ACREAGE, 1860

	MEAN IMPROVED ACREAGE	MEDIAN IMPROVED ACREAGE	GINI COEFFICIENT
Piedmont	158.3	75.0	.582
Sand Hills	97.0	50.0	.571
Valley	105.1	55.0	.566
Western Upland	81.9	50.0	.537
Black Prairie	204.8	125.0	.556
Brown Loam	162.7	75.0	.589
Central Plain	161.4	80.0	.593
Coastal Plain	87.8	50.0	.528
Alluvial	209.7	70.0	.672
Cotton South	135.9	70.6	.602
Illinois	92.1	73.5	.458
Indiana	65.0	50.9	.426
Iowa	63.5	47.1	.433
Minnesota	30.9	26.5	.263
Ohio	72.2	64.8	.345
Wisconsin	54.5	41.8	.398
Northwest [a]	64.5	49.3	.425

[a] Northwest = Illinois, Indiana, Iowa, Kansas, Michigan, Minnesota, Missouri, Ohio, Wisconsin.

parent, in another sense it is equally important not to lose sight of the essential unity of the Cotton South, of the relationship of these parts to each other. In every part of the Cotton South one could find slave-using cotton farms, and in every section one could find small slaveless farms, many of which grew little or no cotton. In every region, concentrations of slaves gravitated toward the best and· best-located cotton land. The "regional diversity" of Tables 2.1 and 2.2 is largely a matter of varying proportions of fertile soils and large-scale slaveholdings—each region being a stratified sample, as it were, from what is fundamentally the same cross section. It is some exaggeration, but not much, to say that the Cotton South was like a stick of Brighton

Rock—bite it off anywhere and the character of the economic cross section was much the same.

For the slaveholders, much of this regional unity extended to the non-cotton areas as well. The essential unifying element was the fact that cotton determined the value of slaves, and slave property was the predominant form of wealth in the South. The importance of slaves as a form of wealth emerges from a study of wealth holdings in 1850 and 1860.

The Distribution of Wealth in the Cotton South

The structure of antebellum Southern society has been described very differently by different writers at different times. The classic works of Phillips and Gray viewed the slave plantation as the pre-eminent institution of Southern agriculture, stressing the tendency for wealth to concentrate in the hands of a relatively small planter class.[15] In contrast, Frank Owsley and his students sought to establish the predominance of the "vast middle group" of independent small farmers.[16] More recent statistical research has tended to be critical of Owsley's interpretation,[17] but variations on his theme have been strongly defended.[18]

The simplest way to characterize these differing views is

15. Ulrich B. Phillips, "The Origin and Growth of the Southern Black Belts"; Gray, pp. 533–36.

16. Frank Owsley, *Plain Folk of the Old South*; Blanche Henry Clark, *The Tennesse Yeomen, 1840–1860*; Herbert Weaver, *Mississippi Farmers, 1850–60*.

17. Randolph B. Campbell, "Planters and Plain Folk: Harrison County, Texas, as a Test Case, 1850–1860"; Fabian Linden, "Economic Democracy in the Slave South: An Appraisal of Some Recent Views," pp. 140–89; Gavin Wright, "'Economic Democracy' and the Concentration of Agricultural Wealth in the Cotton South, 1850–1860."

18. Forrest McDonald and Grady McWhiney stress the independence and persistence of small-scale herdsmen or "drovers," as opposed to "dirt farmers": "The Antebellum Southern Herdsman: A Reinterpretation." Otto Olsen argues that slaveownership was in fact widespread by modern standards: "Historians and the Extent of Slave Ownership in the Southern United States."

to say that the Owsley group focuses on the numerical majority of the small- and medium-scale farmers, while the critics stress the disproportionate shares of land and wealth held by the large planters. The divergence between the two conceptions is shown by the figures on mean and median improved acreage in Table 2.2: the median indicates the size of a typical farm, that acreage which is exceeded by precisely one-half of the farms in the region; alternatively, the mean— which is simply the total improved acreage divided by the number of farms—gives heavy weight to the large landholdings of a few plantations. If we compare the median improved acreage of farms in the cotton belt with that of farms in the Northern United States, we find surprisingly little difference. In an older state like Ohio, the typical farm was actually somewhat larger than the typical farm in the small-farm regions of the Cotton South. However, the average farm size in the Cotton South is double that of the Northwest. The overall degree of concentration in landholdings, as measured by the Gini coefficient of inequality, is substantially greater in *every one* of the cotton regions than in any of the Northern states.[19]

What seems to be true is that the distribution is not actually very different between the two regions in the lower range of farm sizes, but that Northern farms faced an upper limit which did not exist in the South. Less than three-tenths of 1 percent of farms exceeded 500 improved acres in the North, and virtually none were as large as 1,000 improved acres. In the South, some farms, though by no means most, were able to expand to a large scale.

Table 2.3 extends these comparisons to cash value of farms and to total agricultural wealth, which is the sum of

19. The Gini coefficient is a measure of the extent to which a distribution falls short of perfect equality. In a Lorenz curve diagram, the coefficient is the ratio of the area enclosed by the curve and the diagonal to the total area under the diagonal. A value of 0 indicates perfect equality; a value of 1.0 indicates complete concentration, which can only be approached as a limiting case. The figures for the Northern states are computed from the Bateman-Foust sample of 21,118 Northern households in 1860.

TABLE 2.3.
DISTRIBUTION OF WEALTH, 1860

	Farm Value		Wealth	
	SHARE OF TOP 10%	GINI COEFFI-CIENT	SHARE OF TOP 10%	GINI COEFFI-CIENT
Piedmont	47.5	.612	53.3	.688
Sand Hills	69.3	.767	71.1	.787
Valley	56.9	.695	59.6	.736
Western Upland	53.6	.647	56.7	.696
Black Prairie	49.1	.648	43.8	.630
Brown Loam	51.8	.653	52.0	.686
Central Plain	52.9	.660	54.8	.704
Coastal Plain	55.1	.667	49.4	.660
Alluvial	65.6	.780	55.1	.729
Cotton South	62.3	.729	58.6	.728
Illinois	40.4	.569	37.7	.526
Indiana	39.3	.575	37.8	.542
Iowa	38.3	.571	36.6	.533
Minnesota	62.2	.739	56.3	.656
Ohio	35.5	.440	36.9	.441
Wisconsin	30.4	.462	30.2	.448
Northwest [a]	39.0	.564	37.7	.534

[a] Northwest defined as in Table 2.2

real and personal property for each farm operator. These figures have certain deficiencies as general measures of the distribution of agricultural wealth, two of which are that the samples are of farm operators rather than the entire agricultural population, and that there is no allowance for multiple ownership of farms; however, on both counts the indices probably understate the regional contrast which appears in Table 2.3. We find, first, that the degree of inequality in farm value is substantially greater than in improved acreage alone. Generally, larger farms were found on more valuable soils. Secondly, the contrast in inequality with the North is even more marked in terms of value than in terms of acreage. Thus, it is not true that "if one could eliminate slave market value from the distribution of wealth in the South in 1860, he could see that the inequality levels in the North and South were similar." [20] Indeed, the concentration of agricultural wealth—which includes the value of slave property—is no more concentrated than the value of farm land for the Cotton South as a whole.

This does not of course mean that slavery as an institution had nothing to do with the observed pattern of concentration. If slavery is the explanation, however, it must be because of the economic effects of slavery, and not simply because accounting practices regarding property were different North and South. That slavery contributed to the high degree of inequality is suggested by the fact (Table 2.4) that slaveholdings were significantly more concentrated than other forms of wealth. Half of the farms in the Cotton South did not own slaves. Before jumping to a "slavery" interpreta-

TABLE 2.4.

DISTRIBUTION OF COTTON OUTPUT AND SLAVEHOLDING, 1860

	Slaves		Cotton Output	
	SHARE OF TOP 10%	GINI COEFFICIENT	SHARE OF TOP 10%	GINI COEFFICIENT
Piedmont	55.6	.752	56.1	.715
Sand Hills	72.4	.836	76.1	.836
Valley	69.4	.845	68.0	.805
Western Upland	65.9	.824	63.1	.756
Black Prairie	42.5	.644	44.0	.647
Brown Loam	53.2	.746	58.6	.745
Central Plain	59.1	.768	63.4	.765
Coastal Plain	57.4	.778	61.4	.765
Alluvial	56.4	.748	63.1	.787
Cotton South	61.4	.793	68.3	.801

20. Lee Soltow, *Men and Wealth in the United States, 1850–1870*, p. 134.

tion of the wealth distribution, however, one should note that the same table could support a "cotton" interpretation: the distribution of cotton output is just as concentrated as slaveholdings, and indeed the two distributions are remarkably similar.

Table 2.5 shows just how close this cotton-slavery con-

TABLE 2.5.

SHARES OF COTTON AND SLAVES BY IMPROVED ACREAGE
CLASS IN THE COTTON SOUTH, 1860

IMPROVED ACREAGE	COTTON (%)	SLAVES (%)
0–49	5.9	3.0
50–99	8.3	6.8
100–199	14.2	16.9
200–399	23.7	26.9
400–599	15.1	15.2
600–799	9.3	9.3
800–999	5.8	5.4
1000–1249	7.1	6.3
1250 & over	10.6	10.3

nection is. The distributions do not just happen to be similar: they are similar because the big cotton growers and the big slaveholders were basically the same individuals. At the small-farm end, cotton-growing was more widespread than slaveholding. Whereas half the farms were slaveless, only about one-quarter grew no cotton.[21] Above one or two hundred acres, however, the match-up is almost perfect.

What is the nature of this connection between cotton, slavery, and the scale of production? Was it the efficiency of cotton-growing using slave labor that caused the concentrations of slaves, or was it the existence of large slaveholdings that explains the pattern of cotton-growing? These alternatives may sound too simple, but this is fundamentally what the choice comes to. These questions are addressed in chap-

21. From the 28% zero-cotton farms in Table 2.1, I deduct the 3% of farms that grew cash staples other than cotton (tobacco, rice, sugar).

ter 3, but note at this point that it would be difficult to find any indication of scale economies in cotton production in Table 2.5. Note further that the high degree of concentration in slaveholding is primarily associated with the high percentage of nonslaveowners: the distribution of slaves among slaveholders has a Gini coefficient of about 0.6, considerably less, in other words, than the overall coefficient for wealth or farm value.[22] Both of these facts point toward the argument of the next chapter.

Wealth Distribution in Historical Perspective

We can get some additional hints by asking whether the pattern of concentration had emerged anew during the cotton-boom decade of the 1850s, or whether it had existed beforehand. On the whole, the evidence suggests that a high degree of concentration existed well before the late antebellum period. Table 2.6 shows that in the aggregate there was no significant change in the concentration of landholding during the 1850s, despite a great deal of geographic reshuffling of farms of different sizes.[23] Table 2.7 shows only a com-

22. Lee Soltow, "Evidence on Income Inequality in the United States, 1866–1965," *Journal of Economic History* 29, no. 2 (March 1971): 825. Campbell found the distribution of slaves among slaveholders to be less concentrated (in Harrison County, Texas) than the overall distribution of other forms of wealth ("Planters and Plain Folk," p. 385).

23. The 1850 data is from a smaller sample of Cotton South farms in that year, collected by James Foust. The geographic sampling of this 1850 sample is not the same as that of 1860, a situation that creates difficulties in comparing the aggregate Cotton South distributions for the two years. For 1850 we are therefore forced to rely on weighted averages of the regional decline distributions, aggregated by Kuznets's method, as described by Robert Gallman, "Trends in the Size Distribution of Wealth in the Nineteenth Century: Some Speculations." To achieve comparability, Table 2.6 through 2.8 report the 1860 figure calculated in the same way; this explains the discrepancy with the aggregate figures in Tables 2.1, 2.2, and 2.3. The Gini coefficient and the shares of the top 10% are biased downward by this method, but this bias applies to both 1850 and 1860. Several sensitivity tests have confirmed the relative position of the two years.

TABLE 2.6.

CONCENTRATION OF IMPROVED ACREAGE, 1850 AND 1860

	Share of Largest 10%		Share of Smallest 50%		Index of Concentration	
	1850	1860	1850	1860	1850	1860
Piedmont	41.1	45.6	15.6	13.0	.529	.581
Valley	53.3	45.3	11.1	14.1	.617	.566
Western Upland	45.5	42.9	17.1	15.8	.529	.537
Black Prairie	40.1	38.6	13.7	12.2	.534	.556
Brown Loam	51.4	44.6	10.9	12.1	.610	.589
Central Plain	53.6	47.1	10.6	12.4	.639	.593
Alluvial	40.9	52.1	10.2	6.7	.578	.672
Cotton South [a]	46.4	45.2	13.2	12.7	56.5	56.7

[a] Seven-region area only. The Cotton South figures differ from those of Table 2.2 because they are estimated from a seven-region decile distribution, in order to achieve comparability with the 1850 sample. The figures for the entire Cotton South in 1860 are as follows: share of largest 10%, 47.4; share of smallest 50%, 12.1; index of concentration 60.2. See note 23 for discussion.

TABLE 2.7.

CONCENTRATION OF AGRICULTURAL WEALTH, 1850 AND 1860

	Share of Richest 10%		Share of Poorest 50%		Index of Concentration	
	1850	1860	1850	1860	1850	1860
Piedmont	44.7	53.3	11.8	6.2	.581	.688
Valley	61.9	59.6	7.3	5.0	.692	.736
Western Upland	60.7	56.7	7.5	7.0	.690	.696
Black Prairie	45.3	43.8	10.6	7.3	.597	.630
Brown Loam	54.2	52.0	7.7	5.6	.654	.686
Central Plain	61.3	54.8	5.3	5.3	.729	.704
Alluvial	54.1	55.1	7.9	3.2	.676	.729
Cotton South [a]	53.3	53.4	8.4	5.6	.644	.678

[a] See note to Table 2.6. The share of the poorest 50% is 5.0 for the entire Cotton South in 1860.

paratively mild increase in the overall concentration of wealth.[24]

The same conclusion applies to the ownership of slaves. Table 2.8 shows a remarkable stability in the aggregate size distribution of slaves by slaveholding class. Despite a very

TABLE 2.8.

SHARES OF SLAVEHOLDINGS BY SLAVEHOLDING CLASS,
1850 AND 1860

		1–15 SLAVES	16–50 SLAVES	51 & OVER	% SLAVELESS
Piedmont	1850	.360	.493	.148	.292
	1860	.269	.494	.237	.434
Valley	1850	.271	.344	.385	.514
	1860	.338	.538	.123	.672
Western	1850	.318	.523	.159	.536
Upland	1860	.344	.460	.196	.608
Black Prairie	1850	.169	.396	.435	.210
	1860	.181	.531	.288	.285
Brown Loam	1850	.139	.275	.586	.280
	1860	.153	.498	.349	.407
Central Plain	1850	.101	.411	.488	.457
	1860	.232	.431	.337	.438
Alluvial	1850	.182	.378	.440	.202
	1860	.068	.264	.668	.364
Cotton South [a]	1850	.245	.412	.341	.389
	1860	.221	.443	.338	.479

[a] Seven-region area only.

24. The 1850 wealth figures in Table 2.7 correct those reported in Wright, " 'Economic Democracy,' " p. 82, which were erroneously calculated. There are special difficulties in estimating 1850 wealth, because the value of personal property was not recorded in that year. The estimates in Tables 2.7 and 2.9 were developed from the farm value and slaveholding data, using the following estimated slave values: male and female, 0–14, $200; male, 15–64, $400; female, 15–64, $275; males over 64, $100; females over 64, $50. See Robert Fogel and Stanley Engerman, *Time on the Cross*, p. 76. A few other modifications of a minor sort have been made.

marked increase in the dominance of large slaveholders in the alluvial areas and a lesser increase in the Piedmont, it simply is not true that this trend characterizes the Cotton South as a whole. The rise in prominence of slaveholdings of modest size is clearly the dominant trend in the Valley, Black Prairie, and Brown Loam regions. These divergent regional structures and regional trends help to explain how Hofstadter could write that "the great mass of negroes [sic] lived on small farms," while Linden found that "the vast majority of colored people . . . were on large plantations." [25] By varying the area and the cutoff between "large" and "small," either conclusion can be supported. A truer characterization would be that the distribution of slaveholding sizes was remarkably smooth and remarkably stable.

Can this description be extended back earlier than 1850? Soltow has documented the stability of the distribution of slaves among slaveholders over the longer period 1790–1860 [26]—i.e., before the rise of cotton to economic importance. The average size of slaveholding did drift upward over time but not drastically (from about eight slaves per holder in 1790 to ten in 1860), while the Gini coefficient (of slaves among slaveholders) shows no trend. Studies of colonial wealth holdings going as far back as the seventeenth century show greater inequality in slaveholding regions than in free-farm agricultural areas.[27] While there are indications that inequality in the tobacco regions became significantly greater during the eighteenth century,[28] it ap-

25. Richard Hofstadter, "U. B. Phillips and the Plantation Legend," *Journal of Negro History* 29 (April 1944): 115; Linden, p. 152.

26. Soltow, "Evidence on Income Inequality," pp. 825–29.

27. The evidence is collected in Gloria Main, "Inequality in Early America: The Evidence of Probate Records from Massachusetts and Maryland" [*Journal of Interdisciplinary History* 7 (Autumn 1977)]; Peter Lindert and Jeffrey Williamson, "Three Centuries of American Inequality" [in Paul Uselding, ed., *Research in Economic History*, Vol. 1 (1976)].

28. Main, "Inequality"; Aubrey C. Land, "Economic Base and Social Structure: The Northern Chesapeake in the 18th Century," *Journal of Economic History* 25 (December 1965).

pears that the cotton era largely maintained a distribution of land and wealth which had been established before the nineteenth century.

But these essential elements of stability should not be taken to indicate that Southern society was static or stagnant. The available evidence does not allow us to identify the membership of the different wealth-holding classes at different times, nor to trace the lifetime careers of typical individuals. Nonetheless, some suggestions of important long-run changes may be found. It is important to note, for example, that the stability of land and slaveholding is an aggregate phenomenon: in the oldest cotton area of the Piedmont and the most valuable cotton areas of the alluvium a decided trend toward consolidation in large holdings is evident in the 1850s (Tables 2.6, 2.8). One might infer that the overall pattern of stability depended on continued access to good cotton land in the newer regions. Such an interpretation is supported by the few studies available which attempt to locate the same farm operator in both the 1850 and 1860 census. Bonner's study of Hancock County, Georgia, found that very few of the poorest farmers in 1850 had improved their position by 1860: most of the landless had become farm laborers or emigrated from the county.[29] In contrast, the small farmers identified in both years by Herbert Weaver in his study of Mississippi had almost all improved their economic position.[30] In both cases the essential missing information is what happened to the emigrants. But it is well-established that small and usually slaveless farmers led the westward migration,[31] and their opportunities in the east could only have been more restricted if this alternative had not been open to them.

There is another important change in the character of Southern wealth in the 1850s. The last column of Table 2.8

29. James C. Bonner, "Profile of a Late Antebellum Community," *American Historical Review* 49 (July 1944).
30. Weaver, p. 71.
31. Foust, "The Yeoman Farmer"; Frank Owsley, "The Pattern of Migration and Settlement on the Southern Frontier," *Journal of Southern History* 11, no. 2 (March 1945).

shows a striking increase in the percentage of farm operators
with no slaves, from less then 40 percent in 1850 to approximately one-half in 1860.[32] In contrast to the previous picture of regional diversity, and in contrast to the general
stability of the distribution of slaves among slaveholders,
this decline in the percentage of slaveowning farms occurs in
almost all regions and in the aggregate. Furthermore, the
evidence is that this is not merely a development of the
1850s but is instead an observable trend of at least thirty
years. The fraction of all Southern families who were slaveowners declined from .36 in 1830 to .31 in 1850 to .25 in
1860. Soltow's claim that the Southern wealth distribution is
essentially stable over the whole period 1790–1860 rests almost entirely on the study of slaveholders, and hence is
to a considerable extent inappropriate.[33] It is true, however,
that the substantial rise in slavelessness is not reflected in an
equivalent change in the Gini coefficient for slaves among
all farm operators: the main reasons are that very small slaveowners did not hold a large share of total slaves (hence
changes in their numbers do not get a great weight), and the
fact that the effect is counteracted by the rise of the mid-
dle-range of slaveowners at the relative expense of the
largest and smallest groups. But the insensitivity of a sum-
mary indicator like the Gini index to such reshuffling does
not diminish the importance of the changes.

The changing fractions of slaveowners and nonslaveowners is important because of the rise in slave values, especially

32. The aggregate Cotton South figures in Table 2.8 probably un-
derstates the increase in slavelessness somewhat, because the omitted
regions were declining in slaveholding relative to the seven-region area
covered.

33. Soltow, "Evidence on Income Inequality," p. 285. Soltow's
discussion of these figures on the percentage of slaveholding families
(pp. 829–31) is unsatisfactory and misleading. He dismisses the decline
on the grounds that "the number of slaves did not increase nearly as
fast as the number of families in the South" (p. 830). Obviously the
increased relative scarcity of slaves has something to do with the matter,
but explaining a development is not equivalent to showing that it never
happened. The calculation on the effects of urbanization (p. 831) is
entirely incorrect.

during the last antebellum decade. Whereas the average slaveholding rose by about 10 percent between 1850 and 1860, the average value of slaveholdings rose by about 100 percent, from about $4,800 to about $9,400 per slaveowner. Slaveowners constituted the wealthiest class in the country by far. The average slaveowner was more than five times as wealthy as the average Northerner, more than ten times as wealthy as the average nonslaveholding Southern farmer. A man who owned two slaves and nothing else was as rich as the average man in the North.[34]

Table 2.9 gives an indication of how rapidly this division was growing. Slaveholders controlled between 90 and 95 percent of agricultural wealth in both 1850 and 1860. Since the fraction of slaveholders in the farm operator population was declining, this share was not in fact rising. But relative to their share in the population, slaveholder wealth was growing rapidly. (See the third and fourth columns in the top half of the table.) The Cotton South was approaching a situation in which a little less than half the farm operators held almost twice their numerical weight in wealth. The lower half of the table shows the same trend in a different way: the wealth of the average slaveholder was growing more rapidly than that of the average nonslaveholder: hence, the ratio of the two was rising, and the absolute differential was increasingly staggering. Nothing in the table argues that nonslaveholders were being squeezed or damaged or immiserated by slavery: but the economic distance between the two kinds of free Southerners was rapidly widening.

The social importance of these changes cannot be underestimated. Otto Olsen has stressed the fact that slaveownership was by many standards broadly distributed in the South —compared, for example, to stock ownership in modern America.[35] He surely has a point: this was no tiny elite enjoying these capital gains, but a substantial minority of farmers, particularly in the states that became the Confederacy.

34. The figures quoted in this paragraph are derived from Soltow, *Men and Wealth*, pp. 65, 138–39.
35. Olsen, p. 112.

TABLE 2.9.

DISTRIBUTION OF WEALTH BETWEEN SLAVEHOLDERS
AND NONSLAVEHOLDERS, 1850 AND 1860

	Slaveholders' Share of Wealth (%)		Ratio of Slaveholders' Share to % Slaveholders in Population [a]	
	1850	1860	1850	1860
Piedmont	94.8	94.2	1.35	1.67
Valley	88.5	85.5	1.82	2.61
Western Upland	90.3	85.8	1.95	2.94
Black Prairie	98.1	97.9	1.24	1.37
Brown Loam	95.5	95.4	1.32	1.61
Central Plain	94.8	95.0	1.69	1.69
Alluvial	99.1	97.8	1.23	1.54
7 Regions [b]	95.1	94.0	1.53	1.80
Cotton South	. . . .	93.1	. . . .	1.89

	Average Wealth					
	SLAVEHOLDERS		NONSLAVE-HOLDERS		RATIO (WS/WNS)	
	1850	1860	1850	1860	1850	1860
Piedmont	$ 6,582	$19,434	$ 861	$1,553	7.65	12.51
Valley	7,912	20,259	873	1,681	9.06	12.05
Western Upland	6,208	18,223	578	1,947	10.74	9.36
Black Prairie	10,408	34,789	760	1,830	13.70	19.01
Brown Loam	10,356	31,233	1,286	2,214	8.05	14.11
Central Plain	9,908	22,226	691	1,507	14.34	14.75
Alluvial	20,916	61,020	752	2,381	27.81	25.63
7 Regions [b]	8,887	25,058	753	1,764	11.80	14.21
Cotton South	. . . . . .	24,748	. . . .	1,781	. . . . .	13.90

[a] "Population" means farm operators.
[b] "7 Regions" figures for 1850 are averages, weighted by the shares of the soil types in the farm operator population.

But is it safe to minimize the increasing barriers to slave-ownership and the growing gap between owners and non-owners in a slave society concerned about its political future? The very fact that Olsen cites in support of his case—that the percentage of slaveowners was much higher in the Confederacy than in all slave states—suggests otherwise, because the weakening political supports for slavery in the border states was, quite appropriately, a matter of grave concern to Southern leaders in the 1850s.

Slaves, Wealth, and Political Economy: The Paradoxes of Southern Society

The significance of these various statistics depends upon an assessment of the significance of wealth itself. Wealth is no measure of living standards, and many economists regard the calculation of wealth distributions as arbitrary and misleading, because, to list only the primary objections, it omits the many nontangible sources of income such as strength, experience, schooling, entrepreneurial talent, and other forms of "human capital." This objection is only telling, however, if the distribution of wealth is viewed as a proxy for the income distribution. But this is not its essential significance. Contemporaries of the early nineteenth century viewed wealth holdings as fundamentally important because of the instrumental role of wealth in human relations. A family's wealth position could determine its bargaining power, its ability to wait and examine competing alternatives, and its capacity to resist arbitrary actions by outsiders. Wealth represented wherewithal in economic affairs, the power to take risks of likely profitability without risking destitution. This strategic importance of wealth was particularly critical in an era when such modern substitutes as credit markets, insurance, and collective-action groups were poorly developed. The social divisions of antebellum America were essentially wealth-holding categories—planters, small slaveowners, yeoman farmers, tenants, and landless wage earners.[36] In a word, wealth was a basic defining characteristic of social class.

36. See, for example, D. R. Hundley, *Social Relations in our Southern States* (New York, 1860); Roger W. Shugg, *Origins of Class Struggle in Louisiana*, especially chaps. 2–4.

If wealth is important because of its instrumental role, it should not be assumed that a very close relationship existed between power and the market value of real and personal property. The ability to survive indefinitely on a backwoods subsistence farm may have strategic importance far beyond that indicated by the market value of the farm. One assumes that power and value are correlated, but they are surely not identical.

The market value of an asset is important in its own right, however, as an object of political and economic behavior. This is really quite a different point. Property values can be strongly affected by political decisions, and basic political groupings and loyalties can be heavily influenced by the lineup of how the values are affected by political alternatives. Because the value of durable assets like land and slaves reflects an expected stream of returns over a long period, this capital-values effect may have a political impact many times greater than any effect on current earnings. These considerations loomed very large in developmental issues such as canals, railroads, and land sales policies, and the same is true for slavery. Thus, the wealth distribution is significant for a second reason as well: its effect on the incentives and logic of political coalitions.

What conclusions can we draw about antebellum Southern society in light of these two dimensions of wealth holding? A review of the evidence makes it plain that simple categories like "planter dominance" or "economic democracy" are not adequate to describe the several dimensions of the Cotton South. Instead we have a series of apparent paradoxes which cry out for explanation.

We have established that holdings of land and other forms of wealth were, and had been for some time, substantially more concentrated among free farm operators in the South than in other farming areas. This conclusion would not be altered if the comparison were extended to the entire population of agricultural areas: the Gini coefficient of wealth concentration for all households in the Bateman-Foust sample of Northwestern townships is .631 (.658 in the

Northeast), substantially below the figure of .728 for farm operators in the Cotton South. It is clear that the latter figure is an underestimate of concentration for the Southern free agricultural population.[37] It is surely an exaggeration to describe the rural North as a homogeneous, egalitarian society of freeholding farmers, but that region was much closer to such an ideal than was the South. So much for "economic democracy."

But there is nothing in this evidence to justify a claim of planter domination of the small farmers in the sense of the exercise of power or control. As we have seen, the pattern of concentration in land is attributable to the existence of some very large holdings, and not to the existence of disproportionate numbers of very small farms. Most of the small farmers were landowners, (80 to 90 percent as estimated by Owsley) and there is nothing to indicate that they stood in any direct relation of intimidation or threat to the planter. As we shall see, the small farms were highly self-sufficient and had comparatively few direct economic relations with the plantations—certainly nothing comparable to the relationship of employer and worker in the North.

To press the point further, note that Southern wealth holdings were not substantially more concentrated than those of the Northern economy as a whole—*less* so than wealth holdings in cities, where large numbers of individuals held virtually no nonhuman wealth.[38] Now of course, this

37. Campbell found that the Gini coefficient for "all farmers" in Harrison County, Texas was .613, compared to .562 for "farm operators only" ("Planters and Plain Folk," p. 385). Gallman ("Trends in Size Distribution," pp. 22–23) found that the richest 10% of all families in Louisiana (outside New Orleans) held 73.8% of the wealth, compared to 58.6% for the top decile in the cotton-county farm-operator sample.

38. Soltow reports a Gini coefficient of .813 for the North, .845 for the South (*Men and Wealth*, p. 103). Extremely high levels of concentration in cities have been found in many studies covering different regions and periods. See Gloria Main, "Inequality"; Lee Soltow, *Patterns of Wealthholding in Wisconsin Since 1850* (Madison: University of Wisconsin Press, 1971); Edward Pessen, *Riches, Class, and Power Before the Civil War* (Lexington, Mass.: D. C. Heath & Co., 1973).

These comparisons are unfortunately somewhat obscured in Richard Lee and Randolph Campbell, "Slave Property and the Distribution of

kind of comparison would look very different if the slaves
were included as members of the population—by treating
slave and slave values in various hypothetical ways, one can
duplicate the urban distributions. But it is not news that
slaves were a submerged, exploited, and largely powerless
class. What is noteworthy for our purposes is the point that
the degree of inequality among free households in the
South, though greater than that of Northern agriculture, was
by no means unprecedented or even extreme by comparison
with other historical cases.

The same ambiguity is found in the political history.
Many political writers focusing on slavery issues and the Civil
War have had the decided impression that large slaveholders
were dominant in Southern politics.[39] Campbell systematically examined the composition of the politically active groups
in Harrison County, Texas, during the 1850s, and found that
"planter-size" slaveowners . . . monopolized public leadership." [40] Wooster's thorough survey of "the people in
power" during the 1850s showed that all Southern governors
were slaveholders (most of them with more than twenty),
and that wealthy slaveowners were clearly overrepresented in
the legislatures and court systems of the South.[41] But this
kind of circumstantial evidence tells about the personnel of
government, not the exercise of power by constituent groups.
Many writers have called attention to the fact that Southern
politics went through the same process of "democratization"
as the rest of the country in the 1820s and 1830s, from
which it emerged with some of the most democratic state

Wealth in Texas, 1860," *Journal of American History* 63 (September
1976). They do not separate rural and urban distributions and do not
mention the exaggerated influence of Milwaukee on the Wisconsin
figures, which they use for comparison. Nonetheless, their evidence
supports the view that the overall regional wealth distributions were
much more similar than the farm-operator distributions.

39. See, for example, Stanley Elkins and Eric McKitrick, "A Meaning for Turner's Frontier"; Shugg, chap. 5.

40. Campbell, p. 389.

41. Ralph A. Wooster, *The People in Power: Courthouse and
Statehouse in the Lower South, 1850–1860.*

constitutions in the country.[42] Some political accounts describe significant involvement and activity on the part of small and nonslaveholding farmers, and it has not been shown that slaveowners were able to extract resources from small farmers by political means, nor, with the possible exception of secession itself, enact any program to which there was significant small-farm opposition. Even on an issue like the relatively backward state of Southern public education—which some writers view as the essential proof of the undemocratic South—it is not clear that small farmers favored an expansion.[43] As Genovese has argued, the case comes down to a claim that nonslaveholding whites did not understand and pursue their own interests.[44] This is a much more fragile, *post hoc* sort of argument than one based on concentrated wealth and power.

On the other hand, the statistical evidence does clearly show the overriding and increasing importance of the value of slave property. Even on issues such as secession, and others in which slavery was directly involved, however, there is little in the evidence to suggest the exercise of power by an elite, as opposed to the intense mobilization of a substantial minority which felt its vital interests were at stake. As we have seen, the concentration of slaves among slaveowners was not extreme and was not increasing. On issues involving the value of slave property, it is difficult to find an important difference in interests between "large" and "small" holders: even a few slaves would dominate the portfolio of all but the

42. Fletcher M. Green, "Democracy in the Old South"; Gustavus Dyer, *Democracy in the South Before the Civil War*.

43. My thinking on these matters has been influenced by J. Mills Thornton, "Politics and Power in a Slave Society: Alabama 1806–1860." The education issue is emphasized by Carl Degler in his editorial comment on Green's article (above, n. 42) in *Pivotal Interpretation in American History* (New York: Harper Torchbooks, 1966), p. 193. A careful reading of Shugg's account of the rise and decay of Louisiana's public schools (*Origins of Class Struggle*, pp. 69–75) shows no evidence of popular pressure; wealthy planters are blamed for "indifference," not for the exercise of power. Indeed, "the parents of poor children little realized what their offspring were missing" (p. 75).

44. Eugene D. Genovese, "Yeoman Farmers in a Slaveholders' Democracy," *Agricultural History* 49 (April 1975).

wealthiest capitalist or landlord. And the minority owning slaves was by no means a tiny one—roughly half in the cotton South, better than one-fourth of all families in the slave states.

Nonetheless, the evidence does contain a suggestion that the rising values of slave property in the 1850s had their ominous side, not because they threatened to make slavery unprofitable, but because they were making slaves too expensive for most Southern farmers to gain a share of the profits. The very forces that were strengthening the economic incentives for slaveowners to retain slavery were slowly weakening the political supports for the institution. Slaveowners as a fraction of Southern families had been declining for some time, and the increasing geographic concentration of slavery meant that in many of the border states the relative numbers of slaveholders were becoming quite small indeed. The political implications of this trend we defer to chapter 5. The point that emerges now is that it was not the division of wealth between planter and farmer, but the division of slave property values between owners and non-owners that formed the cutting edge of Southern political economy in the 1850s.

3

The Microeconomics of Plantation and Farm

Before we can explore the economic effects of slavery, we have to know how a free labor system works. Since antebellum times, analysts have been fascinated with theoretical aspects of such a comparison, generally taking as a point of reference the contrast between slavery and a competitive free labor market, i.e., a wage system.[1] But slavery arose in a context in which a wage labor system was impossible, and for this reason it is historically inappropriate to juxtapose the two. If slavery had not existed, the alternative was the family farm, and free family farms were not governed by the same economic principles as slavery or wage labor. This chapter

1. The classic statements of this type were proslavery apologists who stressed the incentives toward benevolence which the ownership of labor provided. See, for example, George Fitzhugh, *Cannibals All! Or, Slaves Without Masters* and the discussion of Fitzhugh in Eugene D. Genovese, *The World the Slaveholders Made*, pt. 2. Economists who have compared slavery with a competitive labor system include Theodore Bergstrom, "On the Existence and Optimality of Competitive Equilibrium in a Slave Economy," *Review of Economic Studies* 38 (1971): 23–26; Robert W. Fogel and Stanley Engerman, *Time on the Cross* 1:232–42, 2:132–33; Jacob Metzer, "Rational Management, Modern Business Practices, and Economies of Scale in the Ante-Bellum Southern Plantations," pp. 132–33; Keith Aufhauser, "Slavery and Scientific Management," pp. 811–24.

lays out a simple model of the two systems. The model is obviously a drastically simplified conception of the historical reality: but the chapter will show that it is broadly consistent with the evidence; subsequent chapters will show that the model provides some insight into the course of change in the Northern and Southern economies.

Slavery and the Scale of Operations

As Parker has written, "Continental North America has offered a generally hostile environment to the large landed estate." [2] In antebellum America most farms were small and most large farms used slave labor. Economists have found the temptation irresistible to infer from these facts that "certain characteristics of slavery itself and of Southern agriculture . . . were favorable to large-scale organization." [3] It is only a short step from this to the conclusion that ". . . the optimum unit cost combination entailed substantial amounts of labor and land, so that there were important economies of scale." [4] As Fogel and Engerman argue, "The fact that economies of scale were achieved exclusively with slave labor clearly indicates that in large-scale production some special advantage attached to the use of slaves." [5]

But all of these inferences are unwarranted. We can't know why slave plantations grew large until we know why other farms were small. A farm does not have an optimal size independent of the conditions of factor supply, and we can't infer efficiency or economies of scale from the observed patterns of farm size, until we examine the terms on which scale could be expanded (additional factor supplies acquired). In this respect the overriding economic fact of

2. William N. Parker, "The Slave Plantation in American Agriculture," p. 131. For a similar statement see Morton Rothstein, "The Big Farm: Abundance and Scale in American Agriculture," p. 587.

3. Lewis C. Gray, *History of Agriculture in the Southern United States to 1860*, p. 478.

4. Douglass C. North, *The Economic Growth of the United States, 1790–1860*, p. 125.

5. *Time on the Cross*, 1:234.

life in early America was the extreme difficulty farmers encountered in hiring non-family labor with which to expand their operations.

There is nothing novel in the assertion that labor scarcity characterized pre–Civil War America. But economists who have attempted to construct models of this economy have typically interpreted "labor scarcity" as "high wages" in a labor market which is otherwise perfect.[6] However appropriate such a conceptualization may be for manufacturing, this is not the farm labor situation described by contemporaries and agricultural historians. There is abundant testimony to the effect that farmers frequently could not find hired labor: farms were dispersed broadly over the countryside, population density was low, information channels were slow, and farm labor markets were at best highly imperfect if they existed at all.[7] This is not to deny the economists' proposition that *some* wage offer would have attracted labor from the far corners of the country—the same is true today of the many small towns without doctors. But the required wage must often have been well in excess of a reasonable estimate of a farm laborer's productivity, which is the most an employer could afford to pay.

The essential reason for the scarcity of farm labor is that farmers preferred farmownership and were able to attain it. Most farmers owned more land than they could cultivate efficiently themselves;[8] hence, they had little reason to hire themselves out to others part-time. The census of 1860

6. See the literature surrounding Peter Temin's article, "Labor Scarcity and the Problem of American Industrial Efficiency in the 1850's," *Journal of Economic History* 26 (June 1966): 361–79, most recently surveyed in Paul A. David, *Technical Choice, Innovation and Economic Growth* (New York: Cambridge University Press, 1975), chap. 1.

7. To cite only the standard works, see Paul W. Gates, *The Farmer's Age*, pp. 40, 165, 275–79; Percy W. Bidwell and John R. Falconer, *History of Agriculture in the Northern United States* (Washington: Carnegie Institution, 1925), pp. 163–64, 204–5, 274–76. Numerous other citations may be found in Heywood Fleisig, "Slavery, the Supply of Agricultural Labor, and the Industrialization of the South," pp. 573–76. This section relies heavily on Fleisig's article.

8. Clarence Danhof, *Change in Agriculture: The Northern United States 1820–1870*, pp. 95–96, 104, 138.

listed less than one farm laborer for every two Northern farms; many of these laborers were in reality members of the owner's family.[9] Those who did work for wages in agriculture were either unusually lacking in skills and enterprise, or, more commonly, were young persons saving their earnings for a farm of their own. By common belief, farm wage laborers were "waiting for a better opportunity elsewhere and took little interest in their present job."[10] Thus, even where farm labor was available, the quality of labor and the terms on which it was offered deteriorated sharply once the farmer moved beyond the resources of his own household.[11] The few observed exceptions to the family-farm scale tend to prove the rule: "Those who tried large-scale farming discovered that it was difficult to hire able and trustworthy workers who were content to remain in that role for any length of time."[12] The large-scale "bonanza farms" in North Dakota during the 1880s died out in large part because of "the difficulty of securing labor during peak work loads"; they were replaced by family farms, the majority of which were owned by former wage laborers on the bonanzas.[13]

It does no justice to the thinking of free households to attribute the preference for owner-operated family farms to an irrational desire for "independence" or an attachment to family farming "as a way of life." However prevalent such "nonpecuniary" motivation might be, there were good eco-

9. Gates, p. 273. There are numerous questions about the interpretation of these census categories: some "farmers without farms" may in fact have been farm laborers, others may have owned farms that did not yet meet the census criterion of $100 worth of output. But there were clearly less than two male laborers per farm in the aggregate. Richard Easterlin, George Alter, and Gretchen A. Condran, "Farms and Farm Families in Old and New Areas: The Northern States in 1860" (Revised draft of paper presented at the Mathematical Social Science Board Summer Conference on Historical Demography, Williamstown, Mass., 1974), Table 26.

10. Gates, p. 274. See also Danhof, pp. 73–76.

11. William N. Parker, "Agriculture," p. 395.

12. Allan G. Bogue, From Prairie to Corn Belt, p. 184.

13. Hiram Drache, The Day of the Bonanza (Fargo: North Dakota Institute for Regional Studies, 1964), pp. 113–14; John Lee Coulter, "Industrial History of the Valley of the Red River of the North," Collections, North Dakota State Historical Society, vol. 3 (1910), pp. 577, 611.

nomic reasons as well. The family farm provided a substantial measure of security—against starvation, unemployment, or old-age destitution. In an era of undeveloped and risky financial institutions, the family farm provided a means of accumulating wealth in a reasonably safe form—the wealth being largely the product of the family's own labor in land clearing, fencing, drainage, etc.—and self-cultivation helped to ensure that the earnings from this wealth were continuous and fell into the proper hands. At the same time, family farming combined security with the possibility of large financial gains through an increase in land values. As Danhof writes: "Speculation of this nature was nearly universal. . . . If large capital gains were by no means assured, the risks of loss were relatively small." [14] Finally, the family farm gave the head of the household a convenient means for controlling and exploiting the labor of members of his own family: "The members of a family were not free. They were bound to the entrepreneur by ties of custom, law, fear, and affection." [15] Many of these ties would of course weaken and perhaps break as the farmers' children grew up, but their labor during the "middle" years could be used by the farmer to "add to his acres so that in middle or old age he could start his sons on farms or rent to others." [16]

For reasons such as these, farms outside the South were primarily limited to family labor, using hired labor only on an irregular and usually temporary basis; the size of farms was largely determined by the acreage which the family could cultivate. The purpose of this extended discussion is to show the contrast with the system of slavery, in which a farmer could purchase freely as many slaves as his money could buy. The comparison is shown in Figure 3.1, where the supply

14. Danhof, p. 104.
15. Parker, "Agriculture," p. 395.
16. Bogue, pp. 185, 287. The desire to give one's children a "start in life" in the form of a nearby farm is stressed by Richard Easterlin, "Population Change and Farm Settlement in the Northern United States," *Journal of Economic History* 36 (March 1976): 45–75. One plausible motive would be the father's desire for security after his children have left his farm, though this is not emphasized by Easterlin.

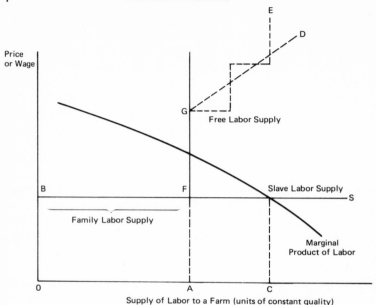

FIGURE 3.1. *The Supply of Free and Slave Labor to a Farm*

curve of labor to a free family farm has a sharp discontinuity at point *F*; the supply curve of slave labor to the farm is infinitely elastic (curve *BS*), reflecting a well-functioning competitive market. The price of slave labor need not be equal to the "price" of family labor, however such a price might be defined; the diagram shows that the essential feature of the curve is not its level but its shape: with land relatively abundant, the marginal product of labor [17] slopes down gently and is very likely to intersect the supply curve

17. The "marginal product of labor" is the change in output resulting from an addition of one unit of labor, holding all other factors constant. Its downward slope reflects the principle of diminishing returns, but if the farm in question owns surplus land, the slope may be very slight. For a competitive firm with only one variable input, the schedule of the value of the marginal product of labor (i.e., the product price times the marginal product) constitutes the firm's demand curve for labor.

in its vertical segment. Under slavery the use of labor is expanded until its price is just equal to its marginal product. From this vantage point, it is inappropriate to argue whether slave labor is "cheap" and free labor is "dear." The essential point is that "free labor" was nonhomogeneous in a sense that does not apply to slave labor.

The presumption that farm size will revolve around the size of the family is strengthened by reference to the dimensions of time and risk, which are not encompassed in the diagram. If a farmer happens to locate a good laborer on reasonable terms, or if a farm has unusually heavy labor requirements (as during the harvest season), we will observe hired labor. But it will be risky for a farmer to permanently expand his scale of operations on this basis, because he will not know how long the labor will stay nor whether it can be replaced (hence the dashed lines GD and GE). As Bogue writes: "The thought of harvest wages was always linked with the worry that it might be impossible to obtain enough helpers when the crop was ready for the sickle." [18] On all of these counts, slavery was different: a slave who was bought, stayed bought; the risks of escape were minor compared to the risks of a free worker's quitting; and there was no danger that crops would rot in the fields because it was impossible to find enough helpers.

A recent article by Heywood Fleisig traces the effects of this microeconomic labor constraint on farm size and factor proportions, in a longer-run context in which land and capital are variable.[19] His argument is illustrated in Figure 3.2. Curves Q_1 and Q_2 are isoquants, showing substitution possibilities between labor and land or capital at given levels of production. The line OC is the expansion path for a farm with no labor constraint, at constant relative factor prices. The labor-constrained farm, on the other hand, can only expand along the kinked line OAD. Obviously, the con-

18. Bogue, p. 154.
19. Heywood Fleisig, "Slavery." We present only the simpler of two models proposed by Fleisig, in which labor is rigidly fixed. All of the conclusions survive, however, under the weaker assumption that the free labor supply is an increasing function of the wage.

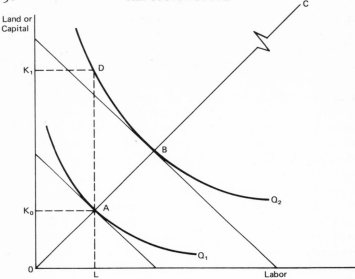

FIGURE 3.2. *The Expansion Paths of Farms with and without Labor Constraints*

strained (free) farm will have a higher ratio of land to labor and capital to labor than the unconstrained (slave) farm

$$\left(\frac{OK_1}{OL} > \frac{OK_0}{OL}\right).$$

The constrained farm will experience diminishing returns to additional land and capital (because of the fixed factor $\overline{L}$), and its expansion will cease at a point like D. The unconstrained farm will use more labor, produce a larger output, and, if returns to scale are constant, expand indefinitely along the ray OC. Thus the slaveowning farm will ultimately exceed the free-labor farm in output, labor, acreage, and farm capital as well.[20]

20. Technically, the result for output and labor force requires only the assumption of concavity; the result for factor proportions requires

All of these predictions are confirmed by the data. Table 3.1 shows, as we have already seen, that average farm size, measured by improved acreage, farm value, or total farm capitalization, was larger in the slave than in the free states. The contrast is particularly marked in the Deep South or Cotton South, where slavery was most prevalent. The lower half of the table shows that the ratio of improved acreage to farm workers, and the ratio of the value of farm implements and machinery to farm workers, are both significantly higher in the free than in the slave states. The critical factor is the labor: the ratio of implements to land shows very little difference between the two regions.

Of course, the regional aggregates in Table 3.1 include both large and small farms in the South. But the suggested interpretation is further supported by the evidence on factor proportions and scale within the regions (Tables 3.2 and 3.3). Despite the fact that the capitalization of large plantations, including slave values, was many times that of small farms, it is not true that the plantations were either capital-intensive or land-intensive, relatively speaking. If anything, the figures suggest the opposite. If we except the Alluvial region, we find that the largest class of slave plantations actually used 30 percent less equipment and land per worker than small farms within the South. Such a conclusion is somewhat sensitive to the rather arbitrary definition of labor and should be viewed cautiously; but reasonable alternative assumptions do not reverse the result.[21] The capital- and

only the assumption of homotheticity; the result on aggregate capital requires only that f_{kl} (the derivative of the marginal product of capital with respect to labor) be positive, and similarly for land. These are weaker conditions than linear homogeneity (constant returns to scale). See Fleisig, pp. 576–84.

21. The major issue is the relative weights to be assigned to male and female slaves. A downward "hand equivalent" adjustment for slave females would raise the land-labor and capital-labor ratios for slave farms relative to free. It is not clear that such an adjustment is appropriate for computation of ratios of this kind, especially for implements. But even an exaggerated discounting of female slaves by 50 percent leaves the land-labor conclusion unchanged, and roughly equalizes the capital-labor ratios for all three slave classes. Fleisig's

TABLE 3.1.

FARM SCALE AND FACTOR PROPORTIONS IN
SLAVE AND FREE STATES, 1860

	IMPROVED ACRES PER FARM	FARM VALUE PER FARM	VALUE OF LAND, BUILDINGS, IMPLEMENTS, SLAVES PER FARM
Northwest [a]	70	$2,958	$ 3,055
Midwest [b]	53	1,767	1,846
Deep South [c]	112	3,478	8,786
Cotton South	130	4,370	11,631
Free States	69	3,200	3,311
Slave States	97	3,337	7,101
Total U. S.	80	$3,251	$ 4,275

	IMPROVED ACRES PER WORKER [d]	VALUE OF IMPLEMENTS PER WORKER [d]	VALUE OF IMPLEMENTS PER IMPROVED ACRE
Northwest [a]	43	$60	$1.38
Midwest [b]	29	44	1.49
Deep South [c]	26	38	1.46
Cotton South	25	36	1.46
Free States	41	66	1.60
Slave States	27	38	1.40
Total U.S.	34	$51	$1.51

SOURCE: Heywood Fleisig, "Slavery, the Supply of Agricultural Labor, and the Industrialization of the South," *Journal of Economic History* 36 (September 1976), Appendix, Table A-1. Parker-Gallman sample.
[a] Northwest = Illinois, Indiana, Michigan, Ohio, Wisconsin.
[b] Midwest = Iowa, Kansas, Minnesota, Nebraska.
[c] Deep South = Alabama, Florida, Georgia, Louisiana, Mississippi, North Carolina, South Carolina, Virginia, Texas.
[d] Fleisig estimated "workers" as sum of farm proprietors, employees, and slaves, converted to a prime-field-hand equivalent using a conversion rate of .39; for the Cotton South, "workers" are free males and slaves between 15 and 64 years of age.

TABLE 3.2.

FACTOR PROPORTIONS BY SLAVEHOLDING CLASS, 1860
(UNWEIGHTED AVERAGES OF FARM RATIOS)

	Value of Implements & Machinery/Labor [a]			
	0 SLAVES	1–15 SLAVES	16–50 SLAVES	51 & OVER
Piedmont	$34.65	$35.42	$28.09	$15.58
Sand Hills	34.30	38.27	21.12	29.12 [b]
Valley	40.50	37.29	35.70	18.21 [b]
Western Upland	42.25	41.09	42.74	23.63
Black Prairie	38.54	33.93	29.00	28.84
Brown Loam	38.76	45.87	38.81	25.65
Central Plain	27.74	27.96	22.94	21.54
Coastal Plain	26.75	32.64	22.98	12.90 [b]
Alluvial	45.86	42.11	67.72	78.27
Cotton South	36.30	36.85	33.00	34.33
Non-Alluvial	36.03	36.67	30.81	24.74

	Improved Acreage/Labor [a]			
	0 SLAVES	1–15 SLAVES	16–50 SLAVES	51 & OVER
Piedmont	38.29	34.08	31.04	26.06
Sand Hills	30.83	26.96	16.57	16.50 [b]
Valley	35.15	38.61	29.64	22.02 [b]
Western Upland	28.03	23.22	20.99	17.65
Black Prairie	25.11	26.56	20.40	20.51
Brown Loam	28.55	29.30	23.11	17.65
Central Plain	36.98	32.15	24.63	25.17
Coastal Plain	28.08	22.24	19.84	25.81 [b]
Alluvial	18.94	17.20	16.02	14.04
Cotton South	30.99	29.01	23.94	20.75

[a] "Labor" means free males, slave males, slave females (ages 15 to 64).
[b] Less than 5 cases.

land-intensity of the large slaveholding classes remain well below the Northern averages. By contrast, however, note the dramatically different relationship between scale and implements-per-worker in Northern agriculture, shown in Table 3.3.[22] Apparently, Northern farms could expand only by use

TABLE 3.3.

FACTOR PROPORTIONS BY FARM SIZE CLASS FOR
NORTHERN AGRICULTURE, 1860
(UNWEIGHTED AVERAGES OF FARM RATIOS)

Value Implements and Machinery/Labor [a]

IMPROVED ACREAGE	0–24	25–49	50–99	100–199	200 & OVER
Illinois	$10.91	$28.09	$51.81	$75.19	$125.00
Indiana	10.28	26.81	44.25	72.46	120.48
Iowa	8.77	26.60	39.84	62.50	111.11
Kansas	10.52	25.32	40.32	66.67	250.00 [b]
Michigan	8.20	21.28	36.23	50.25	......
Ohio	7.05	29.07	49.50	79.37	111.11 [b]
Wisconsin	11.29	28.65	50.51	71.94	109.89
Northwest	9.48	26.32	45.87	72.99	120.48
Midwest	9.87	26.11	47.39	74.63	125.00

[a] "Labor" means males, ages 15 to 64.
[b] Less than 5 cases.

of machinery, but this was not the case in the South.

The analysis is not based on a claim that slaves "could not handle tools." [23] For that kind of argument, even one counterexample such as the Alluvial region would suffice. Nor do we assert that slave labor was "cheap" relative to the cost

---

figures contain a very drastic adjustment of this kind, and his conclusions would be even stronger if he had been less conservative.

22. Of course, the measurement of farm labor is much less certain in the Northern states, but no reasonable amount of hired labor could reverse the pattern of Table 3.3.

23. Eugene D. Genovese, The Political Economy of Slavery (New York: Pantheon, 1965), pp. 54–61; Gates, pp. 291, 294; John H. Moore, Agriculture in Antebellum Mississippi, p. 41.

of machinery in the South. Instead, the intensive use of farm implements in Northern agriculture fulfilled a function for which slavery was a direct substitute: both served to expand the acreage and production of a family farm.

It should now be clear why the existence of large plantations under slavery carries no presumption that these were more efficient than small Southern or Northern farms, nor that there were significant scale economies in cotton cultivation using slave labor. Conversely, the absence of efficiency advantages does not imply that plantations achieved their size for noneconomic reasons, nor by the exercise of economic or political power in cotton, land, capital, or labor markets—except, of course, over the slaves themselves. A fundamental feature of slavery was that it provided an elastic supply of labor to the individual farm, allowing indefinite expansion even at a constant efficiency or constant returns to scale. Such expansion was not possible in the free states because of the unwillingness of farmers to work as farm employees on a permanent basis.

Slavery and the Choice of Crops

But the slave plantation was not simply a scale-enlargement of the small Southern family farm. Factor proportions did not differ markedly, but the composition of output varied systematically with farm size and slaveholding. As Table 3.4 shows, in every part of the Cotton South large slaveholding plantations devoted a much larger fraction of their resources to cotton production than did smaller farms. When output is valued at market prices, cotton comprised about one-quarter of the output of typical slaveless farms, but three-fifths or more for the largest slaveholding cotton plantations. In the cotton belt, these figures essentially reflect the choice between a cash crop and nonmarket food crops for on-farm consumption, the most important of which was corn. The pattern displayed in Table 3.4 is systematic, pervasive, and critically important; yet, remarkably, its presence and sig-

TABLE 3.4.
Output Mix by Slaveholding Class, 1860
(Unweighted Averages of Farm Ratios)

Value of Cotton/Value of Crop Outputs

	0 SLAVES	1–15 SLAVES	16–50 SLAVES	51 & OVER
Piedmont	.247	.342	.485	.537
Sand Hills	.212	.329	.430	.539 [a]
Valley	.188	.303	.387	.644 [a]
Western Upland	.309	.390	.546	.669
Black Prairie	.400	.485	.635	.613
Brown Loam	.299	.390	.591	.655
Central Plain	.288	.362	.467	.604
Coastal Plain	.208	.272	.392	.205 [a]
Alluvial	.228	.483	.606	.706
Cotton South	.252	.348	.508	.616

SOURCES: Arthur H. Cole, Wholesale Commodity Prices 1700–1861 Supplement (Cambridge: Harvard University Press, 1938); Roger Ransom and Richard Sutch, One Kind of Freedom (New York: Cambridge University Press, 1977), Appendix A.
NOTE: Cotton valued at 10¢ per pound; corn at 80¢ per bushel; peas and beans at 60¢ per bushel; sweet potatoes at 50¢ per bushel; wheat at $1.30 per bushel.
[a] Less than 5 cases.

nificance has escaped several leading scholars in specialized works. It just isn't true, as Sam Bowers Hilliard suggests, that "small holdings within the cotton belt concentrated on cotton almost as markedly as did the planters," nor that "landholding size was much less significant than location in determining corn/cotton ratios." [24]

24. Sam Bowers Hilliard, Hog Meat and Hoecake, p. 151. Hilliard reaches this misleading conclusion by largely comparing maps of cotton and corn output: the corn map is dominated by non-cotton areas, which obviously have high corn-cotton ratios. Hilliard also relies on Moore's opinion that "the small Mississippi farm was essentially a cotton plantation, lacking only the Negro slaves" (Agriculture in Antebellum Mississippi, pp. 64–65). This judgment was not based on statistical evidence.

In a notable article on the self-sufficiency question, Robert Gallman showed that food production on typical large plantations exceeded generously estimated consumption requirements.[25] Gallman's primary focus was not on the overall composition of output but on levels of food production relative to farm population. In these terms, per capita grain output was by no means lower as a rule on plantations than on small farms (as illustrated in the lower half of Table 3.5),[26] though the largest plantations were typically somewhat below average. Gallman looked most closely at the largest plantations, and within this group he found no pattern of specialization between the two kinds of crops. Instead, cotton and corn tended to be positively associated, and Gallman concluded that plantations "typically sought self-sufficiency." He went on to explain this choice by noting that the planting of cotton was primarily governed by the cotton *picking* capacity of the plantation. Since slave rental markets were thin and land was cheap, planters "could grow corn without reducing cotton capacity," i.e., at little real cost in terms of opportunities foregone. "It is not sur-

25. Robert E. Gallman, "Self-Sufficiency in the Cotton Economy of the Antebellum South."
26. Gallman noted ("Self-Sufficiency," pp. 6–7) that the *smallest* free farms produced *less* grain per capita than large plantations. This finding has misled some scholars into the belief that small farms were "less self-sufficient" than plantations (William W. Brown and Morgan O. Reynolds, "Debt Peonage Re-examined," *Journal of Economic History* [December 1973]: 869), a result which is impossible because of the small production of cash crops on these farms. Gallman measured only grain outputs, omitting sweet potatoes, a significant food item in which large plantations were laggard. It may be that the smallest free farmers were consuming less corn per capita than did slave plantations, but small and slaveless farms held 30 percent larger inventories of swine than the largest plantations. The figures probably reflect a greater dependence by small farmers on mast and grass (rather than grain) for animal feed. (Gallman, "Self-Sufficiency," pp. 12, 17; Forrest McDonald and Grady McWhiney, "The Antebellum Southern Herdsman: A Reinterpretation," pp. 154, 159.) On the whole, then, it seems fair to say that per capita food output was about the same on small and large farms. The figures for 1850 are similar, except that Black Prairie is no longer atypical.

TABLE 3.5.
FARM POPULATION AND CORN OUTPUT
BY SLAVEHOLDING CLASS, 1860
(UNWEIGHTED AVERAGES OF FARM RATIOS)

| | Farm Population/Improved Acres | | | |
	0 SLAVES	1–15 SLAVES	16–50 SLAVES	51 & OVER
Piedmont	.182	.128	.100	.115
Sand Hills	.208	.173	.349	.126 [a]
Valley	.227	.120	.083	.101 [a]
Western Upland	.252	.195	.141	.133
Black Prairie	.231	.161	.127	.097
Brown Loam	.220	.145	.173	.130
Central Plain	.217	.137	.124	.098
Coastal Plain	.229	.184	.161	.083 [a]
Alluvial	.351	.204	.157	.233
Cotton South	.225	.153	.133	.119

| | Food Crops (Corn-Bushel Equivalents/Farm Population) | | | |
	0 SLAVES	1–15 SLAVES	16–50 SLAVES	51 & OVER
Piedmont	51.4	57.4	46.0	39.0
Sand Hills	54.0	41.9	47.0	43.7 [a]
Valley	66.7	90.9	132.3	41.5 [a]
Western Upland	57.1	59.7	59.9	50.4
Black Prairie	40.7	61.0	65.5	77.5
Brown Loam	67.5	54.5	64.4	55.7
Central Plain	56.6	62.4	57.3	54.0
Coastal Plain	51.9	60.2	45.6	86.7 [a]
Alluvial	50.8	72.1	48.2	51.3
Cotton South	55.8	62.0	57.9	48.2

SOURCES: Weights from Gallman, "Self-Sufficiency," p. 7; Ransom and Sutch, *One Kind of Freedom*, Appendix A.
NOTE: Non-corn food crops are added with the following coefficients: wheat, 1.125; peas and beans, 1.285; sweet potatoes, 0.595.
[a] Less than 5 cases.

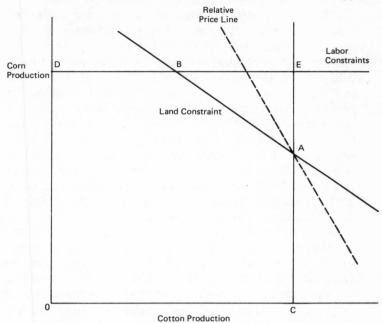

FIGURE 3.3. *The Choice Between Cotton and Corn*

prising, under the circumstances, that it normally paid to produce corn and that planters knew it." [27]

This hypothesis deserves close scrutiny. The simplest version is depicted in Figure 3.3, which shows a production-possibility curve (or opportunity set) for a farm producing cotton and corn with fixed amounts of land and labor. By hypothesis, the labor constraints are non-competitive because cotton is constrained by picking capacity at the level OC, and corn's labor requirements do not interfere with cotton's peak labor demand. If improved acreage were superabundant (no land constraint), production of cotton and corn would always occur in fixed proportions at a point

27. Gallman, "Self-Sufficiency," pp. 19–23. For a similar argument, see Raymond C. Battalio and John Kagel, "The Structure of Antebellum Southern Agriculture," pp. 33–34.

like *E*. Good improved cotton acreage was not superabundant, however, so that most farms additionally faced a land constraint (*AB*), by which the two crops were competitive: land planted in corn could not also be planted in cotton. Thus, the opportunity set is the kinked line *CABD*, and under a wide range of plausible relative prices, the profit-maximizing choice will be a point like A, involving production of both cotton and corn. At A, the planter may be said to "make all the cotton he can, and as much provisions as is not inconsistent with the largest possible cotton crop." [28] Nothing in the analysis indicates that corn production should be at precisely the level of self-sufficiency, but if land is relatively abundant the corn output AC is likely to exceed the farm's own requirements.

There is substantial evidence that Figure 3.3 is a fair representation of the technical choices in nineteenth-century cotton farming. The postwar discussions of the choice of crops were invariably couched in terms of land allocation, i.e., the costs and returns *per acre*.[29] The advantage of food crops was said to be that "they use the same labor which is employed on cotton, but at seasons which do not interfere." [30] Intensive studies of labor allocations over the year show clearly cotton's peak requirements in the fall harvest, and corn's peaks on either side of cotton's in planting, cultivation and harvest.[31] The pattern is shown very strikingly in the following figures on labor requirements on Kollock's plantation, Georgia, in 1860: [32]

---

28. *Southern Cultivator* 18 (January 1861): 10.
29. U.S. Department of Agriculture, *The Cost of Cotton Production*, Division of Statistics, Miscellaneous Series, Bulletin no. 16 (Washington, D.C., 1899); Texas Agricultural Experiment Station, *Cost of Cotton Production and Profit Per Acre*, Bulletin no. 26 (Bryan, Texas: March 1893).
30. *USDA Annual Report* (1876), p. 149.
31. See particularly Ralph V. Anderson, "Labor Utilization and Productivity, Diversification and Self-Sufficiency, Southern Plantations, 1800–1840" (Ph.D. diss., University of North Carolina, 1974), pp. 53–68, 75–81, 263–74.
32. These figures are collected and graphed by Metzer, p. 130.

Man-Days per Working Day

	COTTON	OTHER CROPS	TOTAL
Jan.–Feb.	22	6	28
Mar.–Apr.	10	20	30
May–July	14	14	28
Aug.	3	20	23
Sept.–Nov.	25	4	30
Dec.	10	19	29

There were wide regional variations in seasonality and labor requirements around the South, but in most places the basic facts of economic life held true as depicted in Figure 3.3: cotton's picking requirement exceeded all other labor requirements and therefore constrained cotton production; and the choice between crops was essentially a matter of land allocation.[33] One can easily exaggerate the "natural" complementarity of cotton and corn—the fact that cotton pickers were not diverted to corn does not prove that the optimal corn allocation would not have been different[34]— but it seems evident that a substantial corn crop was "not inconsistent with the largest possible cotton crop."

This formulation highlights several important aspects of the Southern cotton economy. First, it is clear that at a point like A, the returns to cotton are largely economic rents— payments in excess of the opportunity cost of the resources used. This means that the high value of agricultural output and the high profits earned cannot be thought of simply as a productive achievement of the planters and their slaves: they were also a function of the price of cotton, and most of

33. John H. Moore, p. 58; Charles S. Davis, *The Cotton Kingdom in Alabama*, p. 66; Ulrich B. Phillips, *American Negro Slavery*, pp. 207–8.

34. In other words, the two labor constraint lines should be joined by a sloped line rather than a single point. This would not affect the analysis so long as the cotton-picking line becomes vertical above point A. A 1939 USDA study concluded that, while there were potential conflicts, "in most years" the two could be grown "without material neglect or detriment to either crop." (USDA Technical Bulletin no. 682, May 1939, pp. 60–61.)

the region had no marginal alternative to that crop. As we shall see in the next chapter, earnings in cotton were dependent on the state of the world demand for that crop. This framework also provides an explanation for the limited substitution between cotton and other crops—not in terms of an irrational attachment to cotton, but because planters had nowhere else to turn when the price fell. Hence the short-run supply curve for cotton was inelastic, as several studies have found.[35]

Self-Sufficiency and Risk

This profit-maximization framework cannot be a complete explanation for the self-sufficiency of Southern agriculture. An equilibrium at point A in Figure 3.3 may characterize the largest plantations, but most smaller farms were producing somewhere along the line AB. In other words, most Southern farms were producing less than capacity levels of cotton output: in the language of linear programming, the labor constraint was not "tight." There are two kinds of evidence for these statements: first, many small slaveless farms grew such small amounts of cotton that their choices could not have been dominated by cotton's labor requirements; secondly, as we shall see, the evidence indicates that farmers who allocated a larger acreage to cotton usually made larger profits than those who planted the acres in corn. It is not true that "it normally paid to grow corn" at the levels which most farms were growing. This means they were not maximizing profits.

Why should farmers not maximize profits? The farmers themselves would have thought the question absurd: they well knew that the results of their decisions were highly uncertain, and in a context of uncertainty, only a fool or a rich man could safely maximize expected profits in the Cot-

35. Peter Temin, "The Causes of Cotton-Price Fluctuation in the 1830's"; Gavin Wright, "An Econometric Study of Cotton Production and Trade, 1830–1860."

ton South. In other words, abandoning self-sufficiency was risky, because households had to eat regardless of the outcome of the season's yields and prices. The market price did not measure the value of corn to the farm household: "If viewed, however, as it is, an indispensible article of food for the laborer, the working animals, swine and poultry, it assumes a vast importance among the leading objects of attention, and much beyond the measure assigned to it at the current rates in dollars and cents. . . . The cultivation of maize on nearly every plantation within this State to the extent at least of its own consumption, ought to be considered a fundamental principle of management." [36]

A more formal statement of this argument is as follows. Consider the two alternative methods of meeting basic food needs: the farm can plant corn for its own consumption or it can plant cotton and purchase the corn and meat required. The homegrown corn will be consumed directly (and in various forms, such as corn bread, corn pone, hominy grits, and corn meal mush) and indirectly in the form of pork: but either way, the most basic choice has to do with corn acreage, which cannot be planted in cotton. Define the random variables x and y as the returns per acre from cotton and corn respectively, expressed in corn-bushel equivalents (i.e., units of food). Then

(1)
$$x = \frac{Ycot\,Pcot - D}{Pcrn}$$

(2)
$$y = Ycrn$$

where $Ycot$ = cotton yield (pounds per acre); $Pcot$ = cotton price per pound; D = cost differential per acre associated with growing cotton instead of corn; $Ycrn$ = corn yield (bushels per acre); $Pcrn$ = corn price per pound. Let m be the fraction of tilled acreage planted in cotton. Then a characterization of "safety-first" behavior would be

36. "Agriculture of Louisiana," *DeBow's Review* 3 (May 1847): 415.

(3)   maximize $E [mx + (1-m)y]$

but only subject to the constraint that

(4) $\left\{ \text{probability } [mx + (1-m)y] \leqq Z^* \right\} \leqq a^*$

where Z^* is the critical yield level per acre that will just
produce minimum tolerable consumption, and a^* is the risk
level that the former is willing to tolerate. Instead of making
"as much provisions as is not inconsistent with the largest
possible cotton crop," the farmer's strategy is "to be certain
to make enough of bread and meat, and afterwards as much
cotton as possible." [37]
    It is evident from definitions (1) and (2) that cotton
is the riskier choice. This is not because the physical output
of cotton was less certain than that of corn—a question on
which opinions differed—but because using cotton as a
means of meeting food requirements involved the combined
risks of cotton yields, cotton prices, and corn prices. The
man who grows his own corn need only worry about yields:
"He is independent in prices. The fluctuations of the market
affect him slightly." [38] Unfortunately, we have no annual
estimates of crop yields for the antebellum period; but we
can get some idea of the magnitude of the risks inherent in
the process of exchange from the annual state-level price and
yield figures collected by the Department of Agriculture
after the Civil War. Table 3.6 shows that during the years
1866–1900 cotton acreage yielded a higher average food-
equivalent in every state, but the standard deviation (a measure of variability) was four to five times as great for cotton than corn.[39] While we have no direct measures of the

    37. *Southern Cultivator* 18 (January 1861): 10.
    38. *Ibid.*
    39. The means are intentionally biased against cotton. Using the
data in USDA, *The Cost of Cotton Production*, it was assumed that all
fertilizer, ginning and pressing, bagging and ties, marketing, implement
repair, and "other expenses" apply only to cotton and not to corn.
For further discussion, see Gavin Wright and Howard Kunreuther,
"Cotton, Corn and Risk in the Nineteenth Century," pp. 536–38.

TABLE 3.6.

ESTIMATED MEAN YIELDS AND STANDARD DEVIATIONS
FOR COTTON AND CORN, 1866–1900
(IN CORN-BUSHEL EQUIVALENTS)

	Means		Standard Deviations	
	COTTON	CORN	COTTON	CORN
Alabama	13.64	12.37	5.48	1.31
Arkansas	36.37	18.90	13.59	2.16
Georgia	13.36	10.30	6.75	1.33
Louisiana	24.71	15.12	8.92	1.57
Mississippi	20.44	14.26	6.99	1.82
North Carolina	20.81	12.34	7.89	1.51
South Carolina	14.43	9.76	6.91	1.41
Tennessee	33.29	20.79	11.33	2.01
Texas	34.75	20.32	18.57	3.53
Average, unweighted	23.57	14.91	9.60	1.85
Average, weighted by cotton output (1885)	22.94	14.82	10.21	2.01
Average, weighted excluding Texas	18.12	13.20	8.01	1.61

key parameters Z^* and a^* the differences in variance are so great that there can be no doubt about the relative safety of corn for any reasonable estimate of subsistence requirements.[40]

40. It should hardly need saying that this is not an argument about the "variability of income" in modern terms, except that economists continue to reveal a propensity for importing twentieth-century concepts inappropriately into a realm where they do not apply. For example, some economists have argued that corn was the riskier crop because the price of corn was more variable than the price of cotton. See Joseph D. Reid, "Sharecropping as an Understandable Market Response," p. 121; Robert W. Fogel and Stanley L. Engerman, "Explaining the Relative Efficiency of Slave Agriculture in the Antebellum South," p. 290. But this high corn price variance is precisely the reason for growing one's own corn.

The crux of the argument is that, in order to satisfy (4), the smaller the farm, the larger the fraction of acreage which had to be allocated to corn. Obviously, for any aggregate target the critical required yield per acre will be larger if the improved acreage available is smaller. It is also true that subsistence requirements pressed much more heavily against improved acreage on small than on large farms. This is shown in the top half of Table 3.5; farm population per improved acre was nearly twice as high on slaveless farms than on the largest plantations. Recall that the figures on labor per improved acre (Table 3.2) are somewhat conjectural, being based in part on the supposition that slave women worked in the fields and free women did not. But the population figures come directly from the census enumeration and are not so uncertain. Hence, even if farms and plantations shared the same dietary standards and the same self-sufficiency goals, the smaller farms would have to concentrate more heavily on food crops.

The allocation of acreage, however, is not only a function of subsistence requirements (Z^*) but of the tolerable risk level (a^*). This level, in turn, will be a function of the choices open in case of a shortfall. For the poorest small farmers, the physical pains of hunger were a real enough threat. But most farmers, including most nonslaveholders, could reasonably hope to avoid starvation, perhaps by borrowing from friends or relatives, or on steep terms from a country store; or, more certainly than either of these, by selling assets. But selling assets, for most small farmers, did not mean cashing in securities, it meant selling livestock, land, or perhaps the farm itself. Any of these measures threatened the security of the family farm itself. Even if borrowing is possible, this too is a threat because the debts will constrain the choices in the following year, reducing the

---

The extreme difficulty that economists experience in grasping the logic of risk and subsistence farming is well-illustrated by Robert McGuire and Robert Higgs, "Cotton, Corn and Risk in the Nineteenth Century: Another View." See the immediately following reply by Wright and Kunreuther.

probability of achieving self-sufficiency subsequently. The problems of indebtedness and small-scale credit relations in the postwar years illustrate well the fears involved and how real the consequences could be.[41] Thus, when we push the logic of the argument to its roots, the most basic motive is the preservation of the family's independent farmownership, and safety-first behavior is essentially a corollary to the earlier argument on labor supply and the family farm.

We can test this model more formally. The hypothesis implies that the fraction (m) of tilled acreage planted in cotton should be a function of the acreage available (IA), of the farm population per improved acre (P/IA), and of the value of the farm operator's personal property (VPP), an indication of the household's ability to cover shortfalls. We have no direct evidence on the acreage allocated to crops, but we can roughly approximate the cotton share from the output data by assuming that relative yields do not vary with scale. A multiple regression of this estimate on these three variables and an index of soil quality yields the following result: [42]

41. Antebellum dealings with "country stores" similarly involved extremely high credit costs and the prospect of continuing friction. See Lewis E. Atherton, *The Southern Country Store 1800–1860*, chaps. 5 and 6. The argument is well put by Paul Gates: "The failure of a cotton crop meant disaster to a small farmer. . . . A planter would be hurt by cotton failure, but unless he was greatly overextended could worry along without too much difficulty for another year." (*The Farmer's Age*, p. 138).

42. Multiple regression is a method for estimating the separate effects of several independent variables on one dependent variable, where the relationships are assumed to take a linear form. The figures in parentheses below each coefficient are t-ratios, which test the statistical significance of each coefficient. One asterisk denotes statistical significance at the 5 percent confidence level, two asterisks denote 1 percent confidence level. For an elementary treatment of these concepts, see Harry H. Kelejian and Wallace E. Oates, *Introduction to Econometrics* (New York: Harper & Row, 1974).

In (5), the soil quality index is the value of farm per acre, corrected (by linear regression) for the fraction of acreage unimproved. The values of m were estimated by assuming that the relative yield was 12.4 pounds of cotton to one bushel of corn.

$$(5) \quad m = .287 + .070SQ - .109** \frac{P}{IA} + .240**IA + .108**VPP$$
$$(0.25) \quad (6.97) \quad\quad (9.97) \quad\quad (4.33)$$
$$R^2 = .096 \quad\quad (t\text{-ratios in parentheses})$$

Each major hypothesis is supported by the regression: each of the three coefficients is statistically significant at the 1 percent level. The use of such a concocted dependent variable is most unfortunate, but we can have some confidence that the results are not simply a result of this concoction, because the regression is almost identical when the dependent variable is replaced by the share of cotton in the value of crop outputs (as in Table 3.4).[43] Nor is the result an artifact of the geographical distribution of crops and farm sizes, because similar regression results are obtained within each of the major soil type regions.[44] The fraction of the variance in m which is explained is not large (about 10 percent), in part because we have been forced to use an estimate of m which reflects farm-to-farm variations in relative crop yields. But it is also true that there was considerable variation in crop choice among farms of similar size. There were many small farms which put large fractions of their acreage into cotton, and we can learn something about the effects of crop choice on profits by focusing on this variation, as we do in the next section.

Before leaving the question of crop choice, however, it

43. The regression is:

$$m = .311 .151SQ - .124** \frac{P}{IA} + .251**IA + .128**VPP$$
$$(0.51) \quad (7.61) \quad\quad (9.97) \quad\quad (4.88)$$
$$\phantom{m = .311 .151SQ - .124** \frac{P}{IA} + .251**IA}R^2 = .104$$

44. The R^2 values range from .08 to .24. For rather obvious reasons, there is a high degree of multicollinearity among the three main independent variables. For this reason, not all three are significant in all of the sub-sample regressions, but dropping one variable almost invariably yields significant coefficients for the two remaining. Further checks on the robustness of these results are described in Wright and Kunreuther, "Cotton, Corn and Risk in the Nineteenth Century: A Reply," p. 535, n. 17.

may clarify the argument to discuss briefly an alternative interpretation. Many historians have viewed the choice of crops as a reflection of the attitudes and character types of various groups of farmers, their "commercial orientation" or their "sensitivity to market incentives." Parker, for example, juxtaposes the "peasant's" desire for a home and the "gambler's" desire for a fortune.[45] Very often the "traditional motives and patterns of self-sufficiency" are contrasted, unfavorably from a development economist's perspective, with the "new criteria emphasizing costs and prices." [46] In terms of this dichotomy, the small farmers of the South are often identified as a "motivationally subsistent agricultural class" quite outside the mainstream of American agricultural progress: "A common practice of farmers in the plantation areas was to raise the minimal amount of cash crop needed to buy a narrow and rigid range of necessities." [47] McDonald and McWhiney, in their effort to establish the prominence and distinctiveness of the Southern herdsman, specifically deny that these men had any desire to emulate the planters in lifestyle or living standards.[48] Owsley maintained that "relatively few of the plain folk . . . seem to have had a desire to become wealthy." [49]

We have neither the evidence nor the desire to refute these interpretations. But to an economist it is more satisfying to be able to interpret behavior as a response to differing circumstances, rather than a reflection of variations in psychologies or social conventions. Other writers as well have objected to the "common and uncritical use of terms such as 'subsistence' and 'self-sufficient'," with no distinction made

45. William N. Parker, "The Social Bases of Regional History," p. 17.

46. Danhof, p. 17.

47. Julius Rubin, "Urban Growth and Regional Development," p. 15. See also Gray, pp. 122–23, on whom Rubin relies. On the cultural contrast between Yankees and Southerners, see Bogue, p. 236; Eric Foner, *Free Soil, Free Labor, Free Men* (New York: Oxford University Press, 1970), pp. 48–51.

48. McDonald and McWhiney, pp. 149, 166.

49. Frank Owsley, *Plain Folk of the Old South*, p. 134.

between the attitudes and the behavior.[50] These critics often point to "remoteness from markets" as the explanation
for self-sufficiency. Recall, however, that our sample is drawn
entirely from cotton-growing counties,[51] and that both Owsley and McDonald and McWhiney assert that distinctive
small-farm behavior persisted within the major cotton-
growing areas.[52] What is argued here is that the standard
characterizations are too rigid: it was not a matter of choos-
ing between a "home" and a "fortune," but a question of
priorities. One need not view the small farmer's attention to
subsistence production as an attachment to a lifestyle or to
his leisure time, but instead as reasonable and prudent behavior considering his limited acreage and resources. The
contemporary arguments for self-sufficiency often involved a
subtle blend of moralism and self-interest: "The farmer who
never buys corn or meat is generally thrifty, his household is
the abode of abundance and peace, and the corn famine such
as now prevails, never troubles him, but on the contrary fills
his purse." [53] Safety-first behavior may not be an indication
of restricted vision or a lack of interest in improved standards of living; to the contrary, the last thing an ambitious

50. Hilliard, p. 13; Rubin, "Urban Growth," p. 10.
51. The variable SQ (soil quality) in regression (5) reflects access
to markets as well as soil fertility. Its coefficient is not significantly different from zero in the aggregate regression (5); it is significant in two
of the soil-type regressions (Central Plain and Alluvial), but in both
cases the other coefficients are not disturbed. Furthermore, the corn
price of 80¢/bushel, which prevailed in 1860 and which is applied in
the calculation of CS, is very much higher than its average antebellum
level—perhaps close to its usual level in the interior. In other words,
differences in transportation costs are by no means the whole or even
the main part of the explanation for the crop-mix phenomenon.
52. Owsley, pp. 52, 76–78; McDonald and McWhiney, pp. 152–
53; also Gates, p. 9. McDonald and McWhiney distinguish the herdsmen from "dirt farmers," but they do not tell us how to identify the
two in the census, and they even cite census figures on hogs in the black
belt of Alabama to document their argument (p. 152). The great majority of these hog owners also reported improved acreage and crops.
One is inclined to agree with Hilliard: "It would be a mistake to take
the term 'herder' too literally or precisely. Very likely most men so described were part-time croppers as well" (p. 115).
53. *Southern Cultivator* 18 (May 1860): 166.

young farmer would want to do (if he had the choice) is to place in jeopardy his clear farmownership, his independent decision-making capacity, his room for maneuver. Perhaps the strongest evidence for this interpretation is that we observe a crop-mix continuum, not a sharp division between subsistence farms and staple-growing plantations. There is much insight in Morton Rothstein's depiction of the South as a dual economy, but it was not a *bipolar* economy in basic patterns of production.[54] There is no inconsistency in the historian who notes that cotton culture "was not permitted to eclipse the homespun economy of self-sufficiency in essential needs," and simultaneously states that "nonslaveholding whites in the cotton belt anticipated the time when they could boast of the ownership of slaves and cotton fields." [55]

As to the alleged contrast with farmers in the rest of the country, neither the behavior nor attitudes described were distinctively Southern. As a New England farmer put it in the 1850s: "As a general rule, however, it is better that the farmer should produce what he needs for home consumption. . . . He may obtain more money from tobacco or broom corn, than from breadstuffs but taking all things into consideration, will he be better off?" [56] Danhof's description of normal farm behavior in the early nineteenth century suggests the link between self-sufficiency and personal advancement:

> The first obligation of a farmer with a family was to supply, in generous quantity, the necessary food, clothing and shelter. . . . Money expenditures were held to a minimum, partly because money was valued most highly as liquid capital and hence as the means

54. Morton Rothstein, "The Antebellum South as a Dual Economy," *Agricultural History* 41 (October 1967).
55. Rosser H. Taylor, *Antebellum South Carolina* (Chapel Hill: University of North Carolina Press, 1942), pp. 7, 14.
56. *Plough, Loom, and Anvil* 4 (1852): 686, cited in Danhof, p. 23. Note that Danhof's citation is incorrect because of misnumbered footnotes.

to self-improvement. Since self-improvement was defined as accumulating lands, a man was judged by his
ability to apply such money as he had acquired to the
purchase of land. . . . The ultimate economic goal was
the ownership of one or more farms of desirable
quality.[57]

Danhof considers these attitudes to be "obstacles" to "a
rationalized approach"; but his own discussion makes clear
that such behavior was purposeful and logical on its own
terms. As Parker notes: "What was truly new to the nineteenth century was the growing commercial opportunity for
'western' crops." [58] Cotton was one of these crops, and indeed the opportunity in cotton predates the opening of the
Old Northwest. What distinguished the Northwest from the
South was that its commercial opportunities were in basic
food crops: "The crops from which selections were made
for production for sale were generally those proven most
useful on the subsistence farm. . . . Production for the market frequently was superimposed on production for own
use. Only in farms near urban centers was production for
own use discarded in favor of a full concentration of effort
on marketable products." [59] The South had few urban centers
and fewer cash crops. Most importantly, the Southern cash
crops were not food crops, but required separate and distinct activity.[60] The very term "marketable surplus," which
persisted in use throughout the nineteenth century, suggests
an allocation by which the farmer can decide on his commitment to the market after he observes the yields and after
the household has supplied its basic needs.[61] Southern farm-

57. Danhof, p. 16.
58. Parker, "Social Bases," p. 17.
59. Danhof, pp. 145–46.
60. The importance of the "dualistic nature of the planter's output" is noted by Hilliard, pp. 24–25.
61. Anne Mayhew attributes the agrarian discontent of the late
nineteenth century to the fact that it was no longer possible to com-
bine self-sufficiency with profit-seeking. See "A Reappraisal of the Causes
of Farm Protest in the United States, 1870–1900," pp. 464–75. For a
related discussion, see Michael Merrill, "Cash is Good to Eat: Self-

ers had to choose before the harvest, and the choices therefore faced them more starkly.

It is a matter of professional inclination for economists to attempt to rationalize the behavior of small family farmers in these ways.[62] Having pushed this economist's argument this far, however, it would be rash and foolish to deny that differences existed in ambition, in entrepreneurial energy and skill, in personal attitudes toward risk-taking, and in the importance attached to independence and security. And the basic hypothesis does not suffer from this concession; to the contrary, it strengthens the assertion that the choice of crops is the essential economic difference between slaveless and slave farms of various sizes. For we can now argue that if there is a class of farmers who actively desire to minimize their market involvement, they will surely be found in the small, slaveless category; the attitude is inconsistent with the purchase of slaves, an act which *ipso facto* implied a commitment to at least enough cash-crop production to cover the purchase price, debt payments and taxes

Sufficiency and Exchange in the Rural Economy of the United States," *Radical History Review* 3 (Winter 1977).

62. The term "peasant" is probably best eschewed in the American context, because it has too many meanings to different writers. But readers will recognize similarities between some of the elements in our characterization of the family farm and traditional descriptions of peasant behavior. There is similarly an economic literature that attempts to rationalize this behavior. A helpful example is James R. Miller, "A Reformation of A. V. Chayanov's Theory of the Peasant Economy," *Economic Development and Cultural Change* 18 (January 1970), which stresses the indivisibility or overhead-character of family labor costs, much like the presentation here. Economic studies that focus on risk or uncertainty as the rationalizing device include Jerome M. Wolgin, "Resource Allocation and Risk," *American Journal of Agricultural Economics* 57 (November 1975); Thomas B. Wiens, "Uncertainty and Factor Allocation in a Peasant Economy," *Oxford Economic Papers* 29 (March 1977). The safety-first model of crop choice has been applied most frequently to Asian agriculture. See Michelle McAlpin, "Railroads, Prices and Peasant Rationality: India 1860–1900," *Journal of Economic History* 34 (September 1974); Howard Kunreuther and Gavin Wright, "Safety-First, Gambling and the Subsistence Farmer," in *Risk and Uncertainty in Agriculture*, edited by J. A. Roumasset (University of California Press, forthcoming).

involved. Whatever his reasons for desiring self-sufficiency, an independent yeoman farmer was not under the financial pressure that slaveholders felt to grow cash crops. The slave-owner may also have desired self-sufficiency, and for some of the same reasons; but it could not be an exclusive self-sufficiency. Thus slave labor, unlike free, was allocated according to marketplace principles of monetary profit, and we do not need to appeal to efficiency to explain the mutual affinity of cotton and slavery.

Economies of Scale Under Slavery

In their recent book on the economics of slavery, Robert Fogel and Stanley Engerman attempted to measure the relative efficiency of slave and free cotton farms, and to test for the existence of economies of scale.[63] They compared an index of outputs (aggregated at market prices) with an index of inputs, and concluded that slave farms were substantially more efficient than free, and that there were significant economies of scale under slavery. If the argument of the preceding section is correct, then it is not appropriate to aggregate the market value of outputs in a study of productive efficiency, particularly not a study concerned with economies of scale. How much of a difference does variation in the crop mix make? A semi-log regression of labor productivity V/L (defined by market values) against the share of cotton in the total value of crop output (CS) yields the following result for the Cotton South in 1860: [64]

$$(6) \quad ln(\frac{V}{L}) = 4.87 - .0004SQ + 1.27^{**}CS - .0001IA$$

$$(0.4) \qquad (26.45) \qquad (1.78)$$

$$R^2 = .129 \qquad (t\text{-ratios in parentheses})$$

63. *Time on the Cross*, 1: 191–96 2: 137–43.

64. Similar results are presented in Gavin Wright, "Prosperity, Progress and American Slavery," p. 335. The only change is that additional food crops have been incorporated, as in Table 3.4. This change has little effect, except that the coefficient of soil quality, previously significant, is now insignificantly different from zero.

The regression implies that the cotton share is a major determinant of the value of labor productivity, and that each percentage-point increase in the cotton share increases the value of output per worker by more than 1 percent. A farm producing three-fifths cotton will appear to have close to a 50 percent productivity advantage over a farm producing one-fourth cotton. This is approximately the difference between the large plantations and the small farms (Table 3.4); yet the regression shows no indication that scale per se has any positive effect. These conclusions are remarkably insensitive to changes in the sample and in the specification of the regression. The results are not attributable to the higher improved acreage per worker on smaller frams (IA/L); if this variable is included, the fit of the equation is greatly improved but the crop-mix effect is unchanged:

$$(7) \quad ln(\frac{V}{L}) = 3.02 + .0057^{**}SQ + 1.28^{**}CS + .606^{**}\frac{IA}{L} - .005IA$$
$$\quad\quad\quad\quad (6.33) \quad\quad\quad (30.88) \quad\quad (39.31) \quad\quad (9.88)$$
$$\quad\quad\quad\quad\quad R^2 = .335 \quad\quad (t\text{-ratios in parentheses})$$

The argument is carried further in Table 3.7, which displays the results of similar regressions for the major soil type regions and slaveholding classes. In every region the cotton share was the decisive variable. The most important feature of the table is the indication that the cotton share was decisive among slaveless farms as well. The coefficient of the cotton share is not a proxy for the superior efficiency of slavery in cotton-growing: the same efficiency was open to those slaveless farms which specialized in cotton for whatever reason, and the crop-mix coefficient for slaveless farms happens to be precisely the same as in the aggregate regression (6). The same effect is present for each slaveholding class in almost every region.

It is risky to rely on evidence from one year alone. As the next chapter will show, 1860 was no ordinary year. It came at the end of a long epoch of territorial expansion in the cotton belt; and cotton output in that year was 15 to 20 percent

TABLE 3.7.

LABOR PRODUCTIVITY REGRESSIONS, 1860

Dependent variable: $ln \left(\dfrac{\text{value of crop output}}{\text{labor}} \right)$

Regression coefficients (t-ratios in parentheses)

SAMPLE	CONSTANT	COTTON SHARE	SOIL QUALITY	R^2
0 Slaves				
Piedmont	4.98	1.40**	.014**	.142
		(7.94)	(1.77)	
Western Upland	4.88	1.58**	.026**	.161
		(9.64)	(2.93)	
Black Prairie	4.28	2.42**	.027**	.333
		(5.85)	(1.19)	
Brown Loam	5.33	0.78**	−.021**	.204
		(3.10)	(4.59)	
Central Plain	5.03	1.38**	.018**	.184
		(8.67)	(1.94)	
Alluvial	4.25	2.75**	.040**	.441
		(5.59)	(3.42)	
Cotton South	5.01	1.27**	.010**	.123
		(17.97)	(4.17)	
1–15 Slaves				
Piedmont	4.83	1.06**	−.005	.102
		(6.51)	(1.03)	
Western Upland	4.47	1.84**	−.015	.246
		(7.54)	(4.39)	
Black Prairie	3.55	3.45**	.008*	.402
		(8.32)	(1.79)	
Brown Loam	5.08	1.14**	.0006	.168
		(4.43)	(0.01)	
Central Plain	4.60	1.72**	−.0006	.238
		(9.99)	(0.08)	
Alluvial	3.94	2.81**	.006	.347
		(5.20)	(0.33)	
Cotton South	4.72	1.48**	−0.002	.155
		(17.32)	(1.43)	

TABLE 3.7. *(continued)*

SAMPLE	CONSTANT	COTTON SHARE	SOIL QUALITY	R²
16–50 Slaves				
Piedmont	4.40	1.43**	0.003	.177
		(5.85)	(0.69)	
Western Upland	3.51	3.40**	0.007	.474
		(8.02)	(0.49)	
Black Prairie	5.22	0.66*	0.001	.077
		(2.15)	(0.67)	
Brown Loam	4.62	1.70**	−0.004	.398
		(6.01)	(1.52)	
Central Plain	4.38	1.76**	0.006	.288
		(6.70)	(0.63)	
Alluvial	2.12	4.71**	0.006	.660
		(7.78)	(0.65)	
Cotton South	4.28	1.96**	0.004*	.285
		(16.35)	(2.31)	
51 & Over				
Piedmont	3.55	2.67**	−0.002	.659
		(6.49)		
Western Upland	1.58	5.59**	0.016	.865
		(7.48)		
Black Prairie	5.81	−0.42	0.003	.017
		(0.43)		
Brown Loam	4.23	1.79**	0.005	.417
		(3.17)		
Central Plain	4.39	1.56**	0.025*	.378
		(3.82)		
Alluvial	4.91	0.90*	0.002	.163
		(1.97)		
Cotton South	4.18	1.78**	0.005*	.351
		(8.08)		

* Significant at 10% level.
** Significant at 1% level.

TABLE 3.8.

LABOR PRODUCTIVITY REGRESSIONS, 1850

Dependent variable: $ln \dfrac{(\text{value of crop output})}{(\qquad \text{labor} \qquad)}$

Regression coefficients (t-ratios in parentheses)

SAMPLE	CONSTANT	COTTON SHARE	SOIL QUALITY	R^2
0 Slaves				
Piedmont	5.00	0.66	0.012	.028
		(1.14)	(0.44)	
Western Upland	4.90	0.020	−0.082	.032
		(0.60)	(0.60)	
Black Prairie	5.28	0.36	0.088	.123
		(1.74)	(1.22)	
Brown Loam	4.54	1.73*	−0.061	.147
		(1.74)	(0.60)	
Central Plain	5.34	0.28	0.103*	.245
		(0.56)	(2.69)	
Alluvial	4.90	2.28	0.135	.178
		(0.33)	(0.42)	
All Regions [a]	5.08	0.77**	0.048*	0.87
		(2.62)	(2.57)	
1–15 Slaves				
Piedmont	4.60	0.98**	0.010	.118
		(3.76)	(0.69)	
Western Upland	4.85	0.12	−0.044	.041
		(0.15)	(0.72)	
Black Prairie	4.96	0.64	0.043	.086
		(1.48)	(1.56)	
Brown Loam	4.81	0.77*	0.045	.216
		(1.91)	(1.64)	
Central Plain	4.75	0.69	0.076*	.153
		(1.24)	(1.97)	
Alluvial	5.53	−0.42	0.020	.019
		(0.45)	(0.51)	
All Regions [a]	4.83	0.60**	0.019*	.062
		(3.41)	(1.91)	

TABLE 3.8. *(continued)*

SAMPLE	CONSTANT	COTTON SHARE	SOIL QUALITY	R²
16–50 Slaves				
Piedmont	4.79	0.35	0.0002	.023
		(0.96)	(0.01)	
Western Upland	2.55	3.57*	0.011	.698
		(2.12)	(0.87)	
Black Prairie	4.48	1.21**	0.050*	.275
		(2.76)	(1.88)	
Brown Loam	5.60	−0.31	0.015	.029
		(0.36)	(0.49)	
Central Plain	5.00	0.42	0.072*	.203
		(0.46)	(1.78)	
Alluvial	4.89	0.67*	0.016	.179
		(2.42)	(0.26)	
All Regions [a]	4.63	0.85**	0.011*	.139
		(4.07)	(1.90)	
51 & Over				
Piedmont [b]	.....	....	....	....
Western Upland [b]	.....	....	....	....
Black Prairie	4.54	1.29	−0.030	.158
		(1.36)	(0.93)	
Brown Loam	−2.00	9.06**	0.039	.875
		(4.77)	(0.39)	
Central Plain	3.77	1.92**	−0.003	.998
		(33.64)	(1.69)	
Alluvial	4.97	0.11	0.025*	.283
		(0.13)	(2.17)	
All Regions [a]	4.43	1.20**	0.002	.175
		(2.99)	(0.34)	

[a] Note that the area covered is not the same as the "Cotton South" of 1860.
[b] Less than 5 cases.
* Significant at 10% level.
** Significant at 1% level.

above this trend. At the same time, cotton demand was at a historical peak, and the cotton price stayed up despite this bumper yield. If the safety-first hypothesis is correct, we should expect the crop-mix effect to vary significantly from year to year. The only other choice for analysis is 1850, a year in which output was below its trend. A regression identical to (6) on all sample farms for that year yields the following:

$$(8) \quad ln(\frac{V}{L}) = 4.92 + .009SQ + 0.50**CS + .00008IA$$

$$(1.84) \quad (4.08) \quad (0.89)$$

$$R^2 = .050 \quad (t\text{-ratios in parentheses})$$

Qualitatively, the result is similar, but the correlation between the cotton share and labor productivity is much weaker, and the magnitude of the crop-mix effect is only 40 percent of its 1860 level. In the regional and slaveholding breakdown of Table 3.8, some of the categories have too few observations to run, but the message is clear: the regressions look similar, but almost all of the crop share coefficients are well below their 1860 levels, and many are statistically insignificant. If we had farm-level data for every year as we do for 1850 and 1860, it is reasonable to suppose that they would show a wide variety of outcomes like the two contrasting cases we have. So if it appears that small farmers were foregoing an implausibly large income in 1860 by limiting their commitment to cotton, the main part of the explanation is simple: they didn't know in advance that the year would turn out that well.[65]

We cannot prove that there were no economies of scale whatsoever, in part because it is difficult to establish a negative proposition conclusively, in part because there are a number of alternative versions of the hypothesis. One possibility is that the optimum (profit-maximizing) cotton share is higher on large slave plantations. This argument

65. Fogel and Engerman raise this inappropriate objection in "Explaining the Relative Efficiency of Slave Agriculture," pp. 289–90.

receives some limited support in Tables 3.7 and 3.8, from the fact that the cotton-share coefficients are generally higher in the larger slaveholding classes. It is implicit in Fogel and Engerman's work that differences in the optimal crop mix account for *all* of the observed differences in crop mix, though it is not clear what theoretical basis this proposition has. It is evident that differences in the CS coefficients could account at most for only a fraction of the observed productivity differential. Furthermore, the effect is not at all regular in relation to scale, and it is in fact outweighed by the fall in the constant term on larger slaveholdings. A second possibility is that there were economies in plantation activities other than crop production. The available figures show substantially lower outputs per capita for home manufactures and meat products on plantations relative to smaller farms. But we cannot rule out the possibility of economies in other areas such as marketing, purchasing, fencing, ginning, and managerial expenses.[66] Such economies, to the extent that they did exist, are primarily variations on the financial advantages of wealth itself, essentially similar to the analysis of crop choice proposed here.

There is another chain of reasoning by which the superior efficiency of plantations is sometimes advocated: Cotton output per capita is higher on large plantations; the small farms devoted a larger share of their output to foodstuffs; yet per capita outputs of corn are not substantially different on large and small farms; since they produce the same corn and more cotton, the large plantations must be more efficient. The premises are all approximately correct (though the largest plantations were in fact somewhat behind in per

66. Metzer documents efforts by plantations to utilize slave labor efficiently, but fails to show any relationship to scale. The one scale effect claimed, without specific evidence, derives from the indivisibility of the managerial input (pp. 143–44). This cannot be the explanation for Fogel and Engerman's productivity figures, because they did not include "management" as an input. The speculative argument that large planters tended to become better managers because they monitored a larger *number* of inputs (p. 145) is an indication of just how far one must strain to find a basis for economies of scale.

capita food production). The fallacy is that *per capita* outputs are not *per worker* outputs. Our figures reflect the conventional assumption that slave women were in the agricultural labor force while free women were not.[67] If this assumption is accurate, then the equal per capita corn outputs reflect significantly higher per worker corn outputs on smaller farms. The widespread use of slave women in field work, at least during the peak harvest period, is well documented; little is known about the participation of free women, except that it was substantially lower,[68] at least for the field crops on which we focus. The statistical relationship between scale and productivity is sensitive to this assumption (though the crop-mix effect is not): a reasonable medium participation rate would produce no scale effect. This may not be correct, but with our present knowledge it is the assumptions that determine the result, and there is nothing compelling in the data on either side.

The ability to put women to work in the fields is certainly a distinctive feature of slavery, one which has been somewhat submerged in the discussion thus far. One might reasonably interpret this phenomenon as a method for squeezing more labor out of a given household, and thus in

67. This is the assumption of Stanley Lebergott, "Labor Force and Employment, 1800–1960," in *Output and Productivity in the United States after 1800: Studies in Income and Wealth*, Conference on Research in Income and Wealth, vol. 30 (New York: Columbia University Press, 1966), pp. 150–56.

68. Russel asserts that "white women and girls of small-farm families also worked in the fields to a considerable extent," but "certainly not as regularly as slave women and girls." See Robert R. Russel, "The Effects of Slavery upon Nonslaveholders in the Antebellum South," p. 115. Fogel and Engerman assumed a positive participation rate on small farms for white females over 10 and white males between 10 and 15, this rate assumed to "decline toward zero with farm size" (*Time on the Cross*, 2: 138). The post-slavery participation of black women in agricultural labor is placed at .50–.67 by Ransom and Sutch, but they cite an 1875 Georgia survey which puts the figure at .28 ("The Impact of the Civil War and of Emancipation on Southern Agriculture," pp. 22–23). The unwillingness to employ white women, even indentured servants, in field work goes back to the 17th century. See Morgan, *American Slavery, American Freedom*, pp. 235, 309.

some sense a productivity advantage for the slave system. But this is not really the essence of the matter: it is not clear that free females on typical small farms did less "work" than slave females, but they surely did different things. From all accounts there was precious little leisure time for the typical farm wife: without attempting to detail the many activities that filled her day, we can broadly describe them as intra-household production and services. Thus, the badly named female "participation rate" is essentially another aspect of the allocation of resources between market and non-market activities, entirely comparable to the cotton-corn issue already stressed. We cannot rule out the existence of scale economies of various kinds, but we can say with confidence that the mix of economic activities was fundamentally different for free and slave labor.

We cannot rule out scale economies completely, but we can safely rule out the possibility that the sum total of these economies was very large. It is difficult to square the existence of significant scale economies with the smooth distribution of farm and slaveholding sizes in the Cotton South. If this is a disequilibrium distribution, it was a remarkably stubborn one. On the other hand, a wide array of farm sizes is exactly what we would expect under constant returns to scale: the case of cotton stands in sharp contrast to that of sugar, where the basis for economies of scale (grinding machinery) is straightforward. If slave farms were more efficient than free, we should at least expect them to increase their share of output over time; if there were economies of scale, we should expect to see production and slaveholdings increasingly concentrated at larger scale. But as we saw in the previous chapter, the distribution of slaves among slaveholders was essentially stable for a long period of time. While the average slaveholding drifted upward slowly over time, a development quite consistent with constant returns to scale, there was no tendency during the 1850s for the large plantations to outbid smaller slaveholders for their property. What changes there were in the wealth distribution were associated with changes in the value of slaves and

TABLE 3.9.

SHARES OF COTTON BY SLAVEHOLDING CLASS, 1850 AND 1860

		0 SLAVES	1–15 SLAVES	16–50 SLAVES	51 & OVER
Piedmont	1850	.066	.388	.370	.177
	1860	.091	.270	.444	.195
Valley	1850	.058	.194	.342	.407
	1860	.182	.285	.402	.131
Western Upland	1850	.112	.208	.478	.201
	1860	.175	.265	.366	.194
Black Prairie	1850	.021	.155	.342	.482
	1860	.034	.187	.531	.249
Brown Loam	1850	.075	.129	.283	.513
	1860	.050	.136	.467	.348
Central Plain	1850	.008	.085	.360	.547
	1860	.093	.215	.342	.350
Alluvial	1850	.055	.132	.392	.421
	1860	.022	.081	.217	.679
Cotton South	1850	.067	.227	.351	.356
	1860	.086	.205	.381	.330
Non-Alluvial	1850	.070	.235	.345	.350
	1860	.100	.236	.421	.243

good cotton land: the owners reaped these windfalls, the others did not, and there is little indication that the basic distribution of production or productive assets was changing much overall.

Table 3.9 presents estimates of the share of cotton output by slaveholding class in 1850 and 1860: there is little support for economies of scale. The overall Cotton South figures show no significant change. Slaveless farms do not account for a large share of cotton output, but there is no sign that they were being driven out for inefficiency. Remarkably, it is the largest plantations which might be considered endangered in terms of their output share. Only the Alluvial region fits a pattern consistent with the existence of scale economies: outside the alluvium, the largest plantations were the biggest (relative) losers. The figures give us some indication that the medium slave plantations (sixteen to fifty slaves) were relatively efficient—but relative to their larger competitors, not the smaller. What the evidence points to, in other words, is not that larger slave farms were more efficient, but that there was an upper bound on the possibility of efficient expansion, an upper bound which varied between regions. Presumably this barrier reflects the limited supervisory capacity of a single manager, most commonly the owner.[69] For the unusually fortunate or skillful slaveowner, this was no ultimate barrier, because he always had the option of moving to the Alluvial region, as many did. For this reason, the aggregate Cotton South distribution is the most fundamental, and it is this distribution that shows the least change over time.

If the size distribution of farms, cotton, and slaveholdings are not determined by productive efficiency, then what are they and how are they determined? The best simple answer is that the distribution of farm size reflects the distribution of personal fortunes in the population. This is not a denial of the possibility of borrowing, but an application of the "principle of increasing risk": an entrepreneur with a given amount of private wealth, who expands his enterprise through borrowing, can only do so at increasing risk of the loss of his own wealth.[70] Because slave plantations, even large ones, remained fundamentally family enterprises (pro-

69. The nature of these limits are discussed by Metzer, pp. 145–47. It is notable that Metzer's treatment of diseconomies is much more persuasive than his treatment of managerial economies (see n. 66 above). Rothstein notes the existence of an "accepted limit on the size of units" in cotton growing, but argues that this was no real obstacle to continued accumulation by an individual, through multiple plantation ownership ("The Big Farm," pp. 591–92). Stampp and Phillips suggest that inefficiency set in at 100 slaves, but our evidence suggests a much lower figure outside of the alluvium. See Kenneth Stampp, *The Peculiar Institution*, p. 44; Ulrich B. Phillips, *Life and Labor in the Old South*, p. 42.

70. See J. Steindl, "On Risk," *Oxford Economic Papers*, Old Series, no. 5 (June 1941). Formally, if the enterprise has an expected profit rate of e, with standard deviation S_o, then the entrepreneur's total profit is

$$pC = eI - r(I - C)$$

where C is his personal capital, I is the total investment, and r is the

prietorships), it is truer to say that the distribution of
wealth determines the distribution of slaves and cotton than
vice versa. As the agricultural economist Earl Heady puts
it in a general context: [71]

> Uncertainty is probably more important than scale
> relationships in explaining the varied pattern of farm
> sizes . . . while constant physical returns to scale
> alone would lead to an indeterminant size, this scale
> relationship in combination with uncertainty would
> allow co-existence of farms of many sizes. "Historic
> accident" is important [because] the private capital
> of beginning farms differs greatly while the equity-
> risk principle applies similarly to all farmers.

The distribution of wealth is, of course, itself the legacy
of the entire previous history of Southern agriculture, including the initial endowments of the early settlers in land
and monetary assets. Quite plausibly, the better entrepreneurs and managers tended to rise to the top. But the distribution reflects many other factors as well. The expansion
of acreage and output for nonslaveholders was largely constrained by the family's own achievements in land clearing
and farm capital construction.[72] The expansion of slave-

---

interest rate on borrowed funds. It follows that

$$p = \frac{I}{C} e - r \left(\frac{I}{C} - 1 \right)$$

and therefore $S_p = I/C \, S_o$. That is, the variance (and therefore the risk
of failure or default) increases as the total investment increases relative
to entrepreneur's capital. This is not a matter of "imperfections in the
capital market," though the principle may well be enforced by the actions of lenders.

71. Earl O. Heady, *Economics of Agricultural Production and Resource Use* (New York: Prentice-Hall, 1952), p. 547.

72. Martin Primack has shown the importance of this "non-market
aspect of resource allocation within agriculture": "Farm Construction as
a Use of Farm Labor in the United States, 1850–1910," *Journal of
Economic History* 25 (March 1965): 123. See also Primack, "Farm
Capital Formation as a Use of Farm Labor in the United States, 1850–
1910," *Journal of Economic History* 26 (September 1966); "Land-
Clearing Under Nineteenth Century Techniques," *Journal of Economic
History* 22 (December 1962).

holding farms was constrained by their access to additional cash, relative to the generally rising prices of land and slaves. Historical accident looms large in this legacy in the accidents of inheritance, windfall gains, and the results of risky decisions: the historical record of antebellum accumulation does not so much indicate the inherent wisdom of risky choices as the actual outcomes of a game of chance, played a relatively small number of times during a period that was historically exceptional. Those who gambled on cotton after the war did not fare so well.

Slavery: Labor as a Commodity

Was slave labor more efficient than free? The only accurate short answer is that it depends on what you mean by "efficient." The argument of this chapter is that slavery did not possess superior *productive* efficiency in the sense of more output from the same input of labor and other factors; nor did large holdings of slaves produce more efficiently than small ones, in this sense. The efficiency of slavery was essentially an *allocative* efficiency; because the supply of slave labor was elastic to the individual farm, factors of production were combined efficiently according to their relative prices and marginal productivities; both the division of labor within the family and the choice of crops in the field were much more heavily weighted toward more profitable activities producing goods for the market. This allocation of resources reflects elementary economic principles of profit-maximization; but slavery thrived during an era when free men and women would not obey these principles and would not put themselves in the same positions.

Several of these themes may be found in an important 1973 article by Stanley Engerman.[73] One important difference is that Engerman views the free laborer as "concerned with the many nonpecuniary aspects of the employment package," and states that "the benefits of scale economies

73. Engerman, "Some Considerations Relating to Property Rights in Man," esp. pp. 47–55.

. . . are to be contrasted with the utility of being a self-employed farmer." Without dismissing altogether the motives connoted by these phrases, this chapter has argued something different: that patterns of free labor allocation were governed by the internal logic of the family structure itself; that much of this logic was of a highly pecuniary nature, reflecting the risks and opportunities of free farm households; that the apparent existence of scale economies is the direct result of the involuntary reallocation of slave labor toward market activities; and that the extent of this reallocation was itself governed by the level of financial wealth embodied in slave property.

Engerman also notes the congruence between the economic effects of slavery and mercantilist doctrines.[74] This convergence is still more striking when we realize that the basic effect of slavery is not to increase total regional output, but to reallocate output from nonmarket to market commodities: for the South, "market commodities" meant exports and an inflow of specie to the region. Our characterization of the economics of slavery fits well with Immanuel Wallerstein's assertion that the function of slavery was to facilitate the flow of commerce in the capitalist world economy,[75] though it is not clear that during the antebellum period the capitalists of the "core" came out better on the exchange than the slaveholders of the Southern "periphery." Wallerstein's interpretation of slavery is rather different from that of this book; but he appropriately urges our attention to the place of American slavery in the world economic system.[76] We turn to this subject in the next chapter.

74. *Ibid.*, pp. 48, 52.
75. Immanuel Wallerstein, *The Modern World-System* (New York: Academic Press, 1974). It fits much better than Wallerstein's own characterization of slavery as an "inferior mode of production" which is "only profitable if the market is large so that the small *per capita* profit is compensated by the large quantity of production" (pp. 87–88). This confused mixture of micro- and macroeconomic variables calls to mind the old saw: "We lose money on every item, but we make it up in volume."
76. Wallerstein, "American Slavery and the Capitalist World-Economy."

4

The Pace of Progress in the Cotton South

Before the war, the South was wealthy, prosperous, expanding geographically, and growing economically at rates that compared favorably to those of the rest of the country. After emancipation, the same region was poor, backward, and growing only slowly and irregularly. But describing this contrast is not the same as understanding the change. One obstacle to understanding is the historical coincidence of three major developments in the 1860s: the Civil War, the end of slavery, and the close of a long period of rapid growth in world demand for cotton. Just as a proper appreciation of the microeconomics of slavery requires a knowledge of the relevant institutional alternative, so the evaluation of postbellum stagnation requires a knowledge of the nature of growth under slavery. It is not necessarily true that slavery was responsible for the growth that came before and the stagnation that came after, nor that the war itself was the crucial historical watershed. The chapter is divided into two main parts: the first describes the sources of growth in agriculture; the second considers the effects of slavery on nonagricultural economic activity.

The Growth of Cotton Demand

From the mid-1820s, the South was the world's dominant supplier of cotton. This dominance rested on unique geographical advantages in cotton growing, and was the decisive element in the development of the Southern economy for more than a century. Well into the twentieth century, American was the "basis price" in relation to which all other cotton prices were figured.[1] During the late antebellum period,

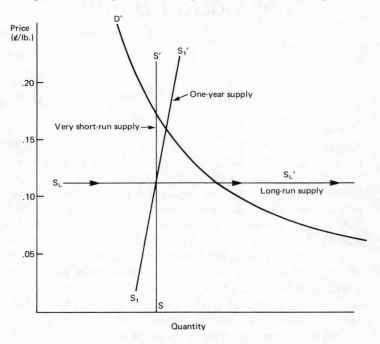

FIGURE 4.1. *Cotton Supply and Demand*

1. John A. Todd, *The World's Cotton Crops*, p. 1. In a sense, the pre-eminence of the South never really ended, but developments in mechanization and irrigation since World War II have shifted the center of production westward into states that were never part of the slave South. Demand conditions have changed primarily because of the emergence of man-made fibers as cotton substitutes.

more than three-fourths of the American crop was exported, and American cotton accounted for more than 70 percent of the cotton imports of Great Britain, the world's largest producer of cotton textile goods. The dominance of American cotton was even greater in the market for short-staple cottons, which provided the materials for Britain's rapidly growing output of low- and medium-quality yarn and cloth.[2] Because of this predominant market position, in any given year the price of cotton was heavily influenced by the size of the American crop.

We can get some idea of the extent of this influence by remembering that the size of the cotton crop was primarily determined by the acreage planted and the yield; during the marketing season, these factors are largely beyond the control of the planters. For this reason we can treat the cotton crop as a predetermined variable, one which influences the price but is not itself influenced by the price in the very short run.[3] The argument is depicted in Figure 4.1, where the very-short-run supply curve SS' is perfectly inelastic with respect to price, although the one-year supply curve S_1S_1' shows some positive response. If we also assume that the demand curve for cotton (DD') shifted to the right at a uniform rate over time, we can estimate the price-quantity relation by the following regression for the years 1830 to 1860:

2. Indian cotton was of inferior quality and sold at more than 25 percent discount. Brazilian cotton was long-staple and not well adapted to Britain's requirements. Egyptian cotton did not become quantitatively significant until the last decade of the century. For documentation of these assertions, see Gavin Wright, "Cotton Competition and the Post-Bellum Recovery of the American South," pp. 611, 617–22; Todd, p. 17.

3. A predetermined variable as of time t is one whose value is determined in advance of time t. In the absence of serially correlated disturbances, a predetermined variable is equivalent to an exogenous variable for purposes of estimation. See Carl Christ, *Econometric Models and Methods* (New York: John Wiley, 1966), pp. 179, 227–28. The same argument appears in Peter Temin, "The Causes of Cotton Price Fluctuations in the 1830's"; Robert Fogel and Stanley Engerman, "The Economics of Slavery," pp. 317–18.

(1) $\ln Pny = 8.21 - 0.944**\ln Q + 0.052**t$
                           (3.64)   (3.58)
                   $R^2 = .323$ (t-ratios in parentheses)

where Pny = the average New York cotton price, Q = the size of the American cotton crop plus stocks remaining from the preceding year, t = time in years, and $\ln$ denotes natural logs.[4] The elasticity of demand, or the percentage change in quantity demanded divided by the percentage change in price, is given by the reciprocal of the coefficient of $\ln Q$. The regression indicates that the elasticity of demand was approximately equal to unity (1.0), and that demand grew at an average rate of about 5 percent per year. Now there is certainly nothing sacred or inviolable about the assumption that the elasticity was constant, nor that demand grew at a uniform rate.[5] But our confidence in this characterization of cotton demand is strengthened by the fact that the elasticity is very similar for estimates over different periods of time [6] and using different estimating techniques.[7] The incorpora-

4. Data are from J. L. Watkins, King Cotton, pp. 29–31, converted to standard 500-pound gross-weight bales.
5. The Durbin-Watson test statistic for serial correlation in the residuals is 0.76, which strongly indicates that the assumption of uniform growth of demand is not really appropriate (i.e., that demand moved in cyclical fashion rather than randomly around a trend).
6. The estimate for the longer period 1821–60 is:

$$\ln Pny = 7.80 - 0.889**\ln Q + 0.051**t$$
$$(4.58) \qquad (4.31)$$

$$R^2 = .371$$
$$D - W = 0.89$$

The fact that the time coefficient is essentially identical justifies the references in the text to a "forty-year period" of 5 percent growth, though one might argue that the relevant expansionary epoch is actually much longer. It is shown below that the elasticity estimate is virtually the same for the period 1880–1913 when growth was much slower.
7. In an earlier study which approached the subject quite differently, I estimated the elasticity between .31 and .65, figures which I now believe to be somewhat low. See "An Econometric Study of Cotton Production and Trade, 1830–1860," pp. 111–20. The present estimates may be slightly too high, because measurement errors in quantity figures and current-year adjustments of stocks in response to price will tend

tion of demand variables such as American and British GNP or foreign cotton production has an insignificant effect on the estimated demand elasticity, and therefore on the estimated average rate of demand growth over time.[8]

The fact that the American cotton crop greatly influenced the price of cotton means that it is a mistake to measure the state of demand by looking only at price.[9] While this point is only the most elementary of economic principles, it has nonetheless been frequently overlooked by writers who are used to looking at the matter from the viewpoint of an individual planter, a particular locality or state, or a small country whose output has no effect on price. The South was in a sense at the opposite extreme: while short-run fluctuations in supply and demand had dramatic effects on price, for longer-run periods of a decade or more price gives almost no information about the rate of growth of demand. Instead, when enough time is allowed for the geographic expansion of cotton acreage, long-run supply seems to have expanded at essentially infinite elasticity. In other words, while the short-run elasticity of supply was low because there were few substitute crops in the cotton area, in the long run the rate of growth of supply adjusted so as to keep the price roughly constant at a level of about 11¢ per pound (in 1880 dollars). The use of the economist's phrase "infinite elasticity of supply" should not be taken to imply that the process was reversible: since much of the adjustment

---

to bias downward the coefficient of lnQ. Thus, it seems safe to place the elasticity between .75 and 1.0 for the antebellum period.

Using the Cochrane-Orcutt iterative procedure for estimating a first-order autoregressive system—a method that accommodates the cyclical character of demand—leaves the result virtually unchanged:

$$ln\, Pny = 8.05 - 0.910**lnQ + 0.049**t$$
$$(5.26) \qquad\qquad (3.58)$$

$$R^2 = .589$$
$$D - W = 1.58$$

8. For various efforts of this type, see Wright, "Cotton Competition," p. 629.

9. This error is made by Robert W. Fogel and Stanley L. Engerman, "Explaining the Relative Efficiency of Slave Agriculture in the Antebellum South," p. 280.

took the form of the purchase and clearing of new cotton land, one would not expect a contraction to retrace the path of expansion.[10] Downward adjustments were painful but during the antebellum period were generally brief.

The significance of this description of the cotton market is that these structural relationships were essentially unchanged before and after the Civil War, at least after American production recovered in the late 1870s. What was new after the war was a drastic slowdown in the rate of growth of world demand for cotton, a development that was largely independent of the war, the emancipation, and all of the associated political and institutional changes of the 1860s. If we duplicate the procedure of equation (1) for the period 1866 to 1895, we obtain:

$$(2) \qquad \ln Pny = 6.93 - 0.614^{**}\ln Q + 0.013^{**}t$$
$$(5.26) \qquad\qquad (2.29)$$
$$R^2 = .769$$
$$D - W = 0.91$$

The regression seems to indicate that the elasticity of demand has risen from 1.05 to 1.60, but this is a minor change compared to the fall in the growth rate from 5 to 1.3 percent per year. As before, the basic character of equation (2) is retained through any number of alterations in specification and estimation.[11] Even if we extend the period to include

10. Evidence for this effect may be found in the correlation between the cotton price and public land sales in the cotton states, and the subsequent effect of these land sales on cotton output. See Wright, "An Econometric Study of Cotton Production and Trade," pp. 115–17.

11. The Cochrane-Orcutt version for 1866–95 is

$$\ln Pny = 6.84 - 0.607^{**}\ln Q + 0.014^{**}t$$
$$(6.02) \qquad\qquad (2.48)$$
$$R^2 = .800$$
$$D - W = 1.86$$

The rate of shift of demand may, alternatively, be measured by the ratio of the coefficient of t to the coefficient of $\ln Q$, which gives the rate of output growth which would just keep the price constant. By this measure, the 1866–95 growth rate is about 2 percent, but no conclusions are affected.

the expansionary years before World War I, the demand estimate (1866–1913) is:

$$(3) \qquad ln\,Pny = 8.63 - 0.910^{**}lnQ + 0.027^{**}t$$
$$(8.27) \qquad\quad (6.36)$$
$$R^2 = .683$$
$$D - W = 1.16$$

In this regression, the elasticity of demand is virtually identical to our prewar estimate, but the rate of growth of demand is barely half of the antebellum rate. As the graphs in Figure 4.2 make visually evident, the change in demand growth was accommodated by a slowdown in the growth of supply, keeping the price stable over the long run, after the transitional period 1866 to 1879.

This evidence suggests the wisdom of Wallerstein's advice to look more closely at the character of the world economy before and after the war. The rapid economic growth of the antebellum cotton economy was no more sustainable than the growth of British textiles production, and the heyday of that industry's expansion was over by 1860. Its rapid growth was essentially the early spurt of a new product in a new market, showing extremely high rates so long as the first wave of displacement lasted, but thereafter limited by the slower growth of population and incomes. As Lars Sandberg, a defender of Lancashire's postbellum performance, puts it: "This earlier growth had been based principally on the opening-up of new markets. . . . It is utterly unreasonable to have expected such progress would continue up to World War I, especially with regard to the growth of output and exports." [12] Cotton textiles, in particular, seem to exhaust market potential rapidly once traditional household and handicraft production has been eliminated:

12. Lars Sandberg, *Lancashire in Decline*, pp. 131, 180. I have juxtaposed two statements without changing their meaning. Sandberg's focus is on the late nineteenth century, but he confirms that the "most important" growth of the industry occurred between 1820 and 1860 (p. 5), and his analysis explains the "inevitable nature of the slowdown in growth" (p. 180).

FIGURE 4.2.
Cotton Production and Prices, 1820–1900

SOURCE: U.S. Bureau of the Census, Historical Statistics of
the United States, Colonial Times to 1957 (Washington:
Government Printing Office, 1960), *Historical Statistics of
the United States* (1960), pp. 123–24, 301–2, 339.
NOTES: Prices are deflated by the Warren-Pearson price
index.
No reliable figures for production during the war years are
available.

British home consumption per head of cotton goods did not
exceed the 1860 level until after World War I.[13]

Indeed, in 1860 the textiles industry stood on the crest
of a major crisis of overproduction, which would have ush-
ered in this era of stagnation had it not been overshadowed
by the Cotton Famine of the 1860s. Cotton goods were
becoming "an unmarketable burden" in India and China in

13. R. E. Tyson, "The Cotton Industry," in *The Development of
British Industry and Foreign Competition, 1875–1914*, ed., Derek H.
Aldcraft (London: George Allen & Unwin Ltd., 1968), p. 103.

1860, and inventories of cotton and finished goods stood at record levels in Bombay, in England, and in France.[14] The real proof of the depth of this depression is the experience immediately after the war: misled by the high famine prices that obscured the demand situation, Manchester merchants anticipated a return to pre–Civil War prosperity as soon as American supplies returned. They found, however, that when American cotton returned, demand for British cotton goods had vanished. By June of 1865, shirtings were "almost unsalable." In late 1866, cotton markets "could hardly be in a more unsatisfactory state"; 1867 was "the gloomiest year on record." John Kelley describes a sequence of events in which every year cotton prices notched a bit lower as American production recovered, and every year merchants looked forward to a return to former times; but each year, the lower prices "did not produce the much anticipated prosperity. . . . The prosperity of the 1850s was to prove rather like the desert mirage, hardly ever to be secured again." [15] Kelley and some British contemporaries place some of the blame on the "loss of confidence induced by the experiences of the famine years." But can we really believe that Englishmen of the 1860s had forgotten how to make cotton goods and money, if only someone would buy their products? And would the "desert mirage" have been any nearer for American slaveholders in the 1860s had the war and the famine never occurred?

Productivity in Cotton and Other Crops

Figure 4.2 does show that the years between 1860 and 1880 are exceptional in terms of output and price, and the foregoing stress on cotton demand should not be taken to mean

14. Matthew B. Hammond, *The Cotton Industry*, p. 255; Eugene A. Brady, "A Reconsideration of the Lancashire 'Cotton Famine,'" pp. 156–62; A. L. Dunham, "The Development of the Cotton Industry in France and the Anglo-French Treaty of Commerce of 1860," *Economic History Review* 1 (January 1927): 292.

15. John Kelley, "The End of the Famine: The Manchester Cotton Trade, 1864–67," pp. 354–65, 373–80.

that the war and the end of slavery had no effect whatever on output. Cotton output fell by half and did not recover to the level of 1859–60 until the crop year 1878–79. Without dismissing the importance of this development, it is worth noting once more that Southern incomes from cotton growing were primarily governed by demand and not by production: if demand is of unit elasticity or less, the South as a region was better off growing less and not more,[16] and indeed it is the case (as Figure 4.2 shows) that the lower output of cotton was largely offset by a higher price during the transitional years. Now the evidence does indicate that the elasticity was somewhat higher than unity during 1866–79, and some part of this rise may be due to the expansion of cotton output during the famine by alternative suppliers, who only gradually yielded their place to the South in the 1870s. For the most part, however, the causation ran the other way: the reduction in American output kept prices above normal, allowing relatively inefficient suppliers a place in the British market.[17] The higher elasticity for these years probably means only that the assumption of constant elasticity is inappropriate for such a drastic change in quantity. Whatever its nature, however, the change in elasticity is of minor importance compared to the end of the cotton boom.[18] When output did recover to its 1859–60 level, the South's market share and the price of cotton were both back to normal: this means demand had gone nowhere for eighteen years, implying at least a 30 percent fall in Southern per capita cotton earnings, no matter what the South had achieved in cotton production.[19] The situation in 1880 is

16. The shape of this curve was a frequent topic of debate among Southern agricultural observers. See, for example, *DeBow's Review* 10 (April 1851): 460; *DeBow's Review* 12 (February 1852). The point is also made by Marvin Fischbaum and Julius Rubin, "Slavery and the Economic Development of the South."

17. These points are documented in detail in Wright, "Cotton Competition," pp. 610–22.

18. *Ibid.*, p. 631, computes the relative size of these two effects.

19. Southern population grew by 49 percent between 1860 and 1880, which we prorate to 44 percent for comparison with 1877–78, the year output reached its antebellum level. Since output and price

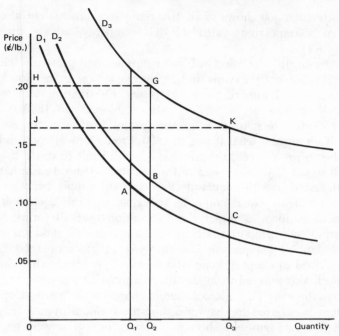

FIGURE 4.3. *Cotton Supply and Demand, 1859–60 and 1879–80*

Q_1 = 1859–60 production
Q_2 = 1879–80 production
Q_3 = Hypothetical 1879–80 production under slavery
D_1 = 1859–60 demand
D_2 = 1879–80 demand
D_3 = Hypothetical 1879–80 demand if cotton boom had continued

described in Figure 4.3: in 1880, output was slightly above the 1860 level, but well below a hypothetical extrapolation of prewar trends (S_s). The fall in output wouldn't have

had not changed but population was 44 percent higher, per capita cotton earnings were less than 70 percent of what they had been in 1859–60 $(1/1.44 = .69)$. If the Civil War had not occurred, Southern population would almost certainly have been larger, and per capita cotton earnings lower, than these figures.

mattered much, however, if the trend in demand had also been extrapolated (area OQ_2GH roughly equals area OQ_3KJ).

Ironically, the effects of lower output were primarily felt in the non-cotton crops and in livestock, where the South exerted no influence on world prices. Destruction of live-stock was one of the major costs of the war: in 1880 the per capita stock of hogs in the leading cotton states was only about half what it was in 1860. Production of corn and other crops also fell, though it is more difficult to relate this fall to the physical ravages of the war itself. Peter Temin has calculated that the demand effect and the supply effect de-serve roughly equal emphasis in explaining the decline in Southern income, under the assumption that all forms of output fell proportionately.[20] If, however, we take as a standard of comparison the crop-mix behavior of 1860 as described in chapter 3, we would have to conclude that the South also suffered from the abandonment of self-sufficiency after the war. The microeconomic character of this develop-ment is deferred to chapter 6, but the regional impact may be seen in Figure 4.3: because incomes in cotton were gov-erned by demand, the South reduced her real income by exchanging cotton for corn and meat, foodstuffs that could have been produced at little real cost to the region as a whole.[21] Through this curious historical coincidence, the

20. Peter Temin, "The Post-Bellum Recovery of the South and the Cost of the Civil War."

21. To be strictly true, these statements require that the elasticity of cotton demand be unity or below. This appears to have been the case, at least after the abnormal recovery years of 1866–79. The demand curve estimate for 1879–1913 is

$$ln\,Pny = 9.51 - 1.03**lnQ + 0.029**t$$
$$(5.20) \qquad (5.20)$$

$$R^2 = .458$$
$$D - W = 1.03$$

and the Cochrane-Orcutt version is

$$ln\,Pny = 9.11 - 1.00**lnQ + 0.031**t$$
$$(6.75) \qquad (5.49)$$

$$R^2 = .612$$
$$D - W = 1.86$$

logic of self-sufficiency applied as much to the region as to the individual farm, though for very different reasons. The postbellum South lacked a mechanism by which to realize this potential, however, and developed institutions which discouraged self-sufficiency at the level of the farm, as chapter 6 describes.

The reason for the drastic fall in per capita outputs of cotton and other crops remains to be explained. Many writers refer to all of this decline as part of the incidence or cost of the war, but, as we have seen, this usage is not safe.[22] Ransom and Sutch argue that the major part of the decline does not represent destruction, but is instead the result of the refusal of the freed black families to work as many hours per year as they had under slavery. They estimate that the black labor supply per capita fell by 28 to 37 percent, the largest component of which is the withdrawal of black women from field work.[23] This loss in productivity could have been expected as a consequence of any serious emancipation scheme and is not properly viewed as a cost of the war.

Whether this labor-supply effect accounts for the whole of the fall in output is uncertain. Apart from this, however, there is very little evidence of genuine productivity gains under slavery which were subject to loss with emancipation. The cross section evidence was reviewed in the previous chapter; the time-series evidence is meager indeed. Fogel and Engerman point to the slow long-run decline in the cotton price (.79 percent per year) as evidence of improvement in efficiency over time.[24] By this criterion, however, we would have to judge that productivity gains came to an end by the 1820s—about the time of completion of the

22. Eugene M. Lerner, "Southern Output and Agricultural Income, 1860–1880," *Agricultural History* 33 (July 1959); Claudia Goldin and Frank Lewis, "The Economic Cost of the American Civil War," *Journal of Economic History* 35 (June 1975): 299–326; James L. Sellers, "The Economic Incidence of the Civil War in the South," *Mississippi Valley Historical Review* 14 (September 1927).

23. Roger Ransom and Richard Sutch, "The Impact of the Civil War and of Emancipation on Southern Agriculture," pp. 13–14, 22–23.

24. *Time on the Cross* 1:91–93; 2:86.

initial shift into cotton out of tobacco, rice, and grains—
because there is no downward trend in cotton prices after
1825.[25] When output recovered after the war, the price was
exactly what it had been before: American cotton still dominated world production, and there was no increase in price
representing the costs of less efficient production under
free labor.

It is certainly true that cotton output per capita or per
slave rose markedly over the last forty to sixty years before
the Civil War, as several writers have noted in connection
with the profitability-of-slavery issue.[26] But it is not clear
how this development is to be explained or interpreted.
Conventional economic analysis draws a distinction between
productivity changes that result from a change in the quantity or quality of complementary factors of production (primarily land), and productivity changes that result from an
improvement in efficiency or technology (total-factor productivity change). Before the 1820s, much of the increasing
output of cotton was simply a shift of acreage out of other
crops and into cotton. Putting aside this very serious difficulty, available estimates of productivity change beg the
question of how the change should be interpreted: typically,
the figures are based on an estimate of labor requirements
per acre combined with an estimate of cotton yield per

25. The least-squares regression line for 1825–1860 is

$$ln \, Pny = 2.38 + 0.0014t$$
$$(0.46)$$

$$R^2 = .006$$

and for the longer period 1825–1910

$$ln \, Pny = 2.55 - 0.0008t$$
$$(0.50)$$

$$R^2 = .003$$

26. Alfred H. Conrad and John R. Meyer, "The Economics of
Slavery in the Antebellum South," pp. 116–18. It is apparently this
gross and ambiguous measure that Conrad and Meyer had in mind in
asserting that "some increase in productivity in the ante-bellum cotton
culture can be easily demonstrated." See "Slavery as an Obstacle to
Economic Growth in the United States," *Journal of Economic History*
27 (December 1967), p. 530.

acre.[27] Now a decrease in labor requirements per acre might be a reflection of improved labor skills or better plantation organization, but the same development may simply reflect the fact that the quantity of improved acreage was growing more rapidly than the labor force.

The difficulty in distinguishing efficiency gains from changes in factor proportions is compounded for the cotton economy by two related considerations. The first is that, as it happened, the average fertility of southwestern cotton land was substantially greater than that of the first Cotton Kingdom on the Piedmont and southeastern Coastal Plain. To some extent the east-west regional shift increased productivity in all parts of the country, but it appears to be true that the differential in natural fertility was much greater in the South than in the North.[28] The second related difficulty flows from the analysis of the preceding chapter: as we saw there, the crop mix was not independent of the ratio of improved acreage to population. As average farm size and the average slaveholding increased over time, the share of cotton in total output increased, as a larger surplus acreage above subsistence needs developed. The crude measures of cotton bales per slave, per worker, or per capita thus give little hint above the extent of genuine productivity gains over time, their character, or their connection with slavery.

The same is unfortunately true for those attempts to utilize census data to estimate productivity change during the late antebellum decades. In addition to the conceptual problems outlined above, these efforts are beset by two further difficulties: first, the yield of cotton was highly vola-

27. This is the procedure of Robert E. Gallman, "The Agricultural Sector and the Pace of Economic Growth," pp. 62, 67–68. Gallman relies on M. R. Cooper, C. T. Barton, and A. P. Brodell, *Progress of Farm Mechanization*, USDA Miscellaneous Publication 630 (October 1947), who use a similar method. Gallman expressly states that he cannot identify the underlying nature of changes in productivity and that his interest lies in quite a different question.

28. Richard Easterlin, "Farm Production and Income in Old and New Areas at Mid-Century," pp. 87–90, 95–97, 105.

tile, and the three census years 1840, 1850, and 1860 were
not at all representative; secondly, productivity estimates
based on an aggregation of crops by market value are not
independent of trends in cotton demand. The first of these
is simply an accident of history: the census year crop of
1849–50 was severely damaged in all the cotton states by
a late April frost and had to be replanted; a series of lesser
misfortunes followed, causing a "failure . . . so great, that
it is almost impossible to expect a like deficiency again." [29]
Conversely, the census year crop of 1859–60 was enormous,
far above the normal trend of expansion and towering over
the immediately preceding and succeeding crops, which
were also very good ones. We can obtain some idea of the
extent of the bias by examining the residuals from estimates of cotton supply curves for the antebellum period:
under several alternative specifications, the 1849–50 output
is between 5.8 percent and 19.7 percent below the level
predicted by the supply function, while the 1859–60 output
is between 11.6 percent and 23.6 percent above the predicted level.[30] The median estimates imply an apparent but

29. *Annual Report of Commissioner of Patents*, 1850, vol. 2, p. 510.
Further testimony appears in the 1849 *Annual Report*, pp. 144, 149,
170, 307, and in Watkins, pp. 81, 107, 150, 197, 217, 240, 258.
    30. The three supply-curve specifications are:

$$\ln Q = a + b\,P_{-1} + ct$$
$$\ln Q = a + b\,P_{-1} + cL_{-2}$$
$$\ln Q = a + b\,P_{-1} + ct + dL_{-2}$$

where Q = cotton output, P_{-1} = cotton price lagged one year, t = time
in years, and L_{-2} = cumulative sales of public land in cotton areas, lagged
two years. More detail on these estimates may be found in Wright, "An
Econometric Study," pp. 114–17, and Wright, "Prosperity, Progress,
and American Slavery," pp. 333–34. Fogel and Engerman's characterization of this procedure ("Explaining the Relative Efficiency of Slave
Agriculture," pp. 281–82) is inaccurate. None of the ratios they mention (e.g., the fraction of land improved, the fraction of acreage in
cotton) are assumed "fixed during the decade of the 1850s." The secu-
lar increase of these ratios is reflected in the coefficients of L_{-2} and t.
The equations track the rise in output during the 1850s very closely,
excepting only the huge crop of 1859–60.
    Fogel and Engerman assert that an exceptional yield in 1859–60
was not mentioned in contemporary comments, but they are mistaken.
See, for example, *American Cotton Planter*, New Series, vol. 4
(Montgomery, Alabama: April 1860), pp. 163–64.

completely spurious productivity growth of 2.9 percent per year, which is exactly the figure obtained from the raw data on output per slave.[31]

The census year 1839–40, on the other hand, was a good year in terms of output (though not in terms of demand): supply residuals range from +7.4 percent to +26.9 percent.[32] However, there are severe problems in using the 1840 census materials. The microeconomic data have not survived, and the published data are suspect.[33] The available evidence suggests that the proportion of cotton to total output was substantially higher in 1860 than in 1840.[34] In an attempt to avoid this crop-mix problem by measuring the market value of outputs, one founders because the demand situation was much less favorable in 1840 than in 1860: demand-side deviations from the trend would account for an apparent productivity growth of almost 1 percent per year between the two points.[35]

Richard Easterlin has estimated the value of agricultural output per worker in 1840 and 1860, using a fixed set of relative prices (1879 levels). He finds that productivity grew by 16 percent over these two decades, and concludes that ". . . the Southern divisions did not do badly. . . . For the South as a whole, productivity grew about the national average." [36] While the use of fixed prices eliminates the effects of cyclical fluctuations in demand, even this most careful productivity calculation is not really independent of

31. James D. Foust and Dale E. Swan, "Productivity and Profitability of Antebellum Slave Labor," pp. 44–45, cited in Fogel and Engerman, "The Economics of Slavery," p. 315.

32. In this instance the specification of the supply curve makes a significant difference: the large output of 1839–40 can largely be accounted for by the heavy volume of land sales earlier in the 1830s. See Wright, "An Econometric Study," p. 116.

33. The useability of the 1840 census data is debated by Gerald Gunderson and Robert Gallman, "Southern Ante-Bellum Income Reconsidered," *Explorations in Economic History* 10 (Winter 1973); 12 (January 1975).

34. According to the 1840 census, the ratio of cotton to corn output (bales per 1,000 bushels) was 21.6 in the seven leading cotton states, whereas the ratio was 30.3 in 1860.

35. Wright, "Prosperity, Progress, and American Slavery," p. 333.

36. Easterlin, "Farm Production and Income," pp. 95, 99.

demand-side trends. The evidence of the preceding chapter showed that at normal relative prices (not very different from the 1879 levels), the value of average and marginal labor productivity was higher in cotton than in alternative crops. Therefore, the relative shift in the crop mix toward cotton between 1840 and 1860 would account for an apparent rise in productivity, even at fixed prices. The important point is that it was the growth of cotton demand which allowed and encouraged this shift to take place. As the safety-first model would predict, per capita corn production remained virtually constant between 1840 and 1860, as most of the newly-cleared acreage was put into cotton.[37] This process would not have continued had not demand expansion maintained the price level despite the growth of output. But if cotton production had continued to grow without a rise in demand, then the price would have rapidly declined, making the application of fixed 1879 prices radically inappropriate in a very short time. Thus, there is no escape: these indices are not measures of physical productivity, and to date there is no satisfactory evidence of genuine productivity gains in Southern agriculture before the Civil War.[38]

37. For the five cotton states, the three census figures for corn output per capita are 29.07, 31.07, 29.58; for the eleven Southern states, the figures are 34.54, 33.41, and 31.47.

38. Easterlin's figures do, in fact, indicate that the apparent Southern productivity growth is entirely concentrated in the strong-demand decade of the 1850s (p. 110), a decade for which the cotton output trend is severely biased as noted above. This result may not be as decisive as it appears because Easterlin finds the same time pattern for the whole country, and doubts the reliability of his 1850 figures (p. 92). The only basis for this suspicion is the implausibility of the resulting time pattern, which seems a weak reason for throwing out one-third of the evidence. As we have seen, the pattern is consistent with the other evidence for the South. Perhaps the same is true of the North, where the 1850s were a decade of accelerated mechanization. However, the census year 1860 was not a particularly notable one for the North on either supply or demand sides, so perhaps the comparison is not quite as favorable to the South as Easterlin believes. See the evidence in Wright, "Prosperity, Progress, and American Slavery," pp. 314–15.

Slavery and NonAgricultural Economic Activity

The foregoing discussion is not intended to dispute Easter-lin's assertion that "there is little . . . to suggest noticeable economic retrogression in the South considered as a whole in the two decades before the Civil War." [39] Neither does it mean to imply that there was a lack of diligence, effort, or skills on the part of Southern farmers, nor that slave labor made agricultural progress impossible. Limits of geography and nineteenth-century science severely constrained the choice of crops in the Cotton South, and the trends in demand were surely not within the planters' control. What is disputed is any claim of unusual productive efficiency or progressive achievement on the part of antebellum Southern agriculture. The pattern of rapid but primarily extensive growth, without major productivity gains, was characteristic of American agriculture generally, at least before 1850.[40] It is really only in the late antebellum period that significant North-South differences emerged in the character of produc-tivity growth.

One of the dimensions of this emerging regional con-trast may be seen in Table 4.1, which records the differences in numbers of patents granted for mechanical inventions in each of three major national crops.[41] In the 1850s, patent activity accelerated in the Northern crops, corn and partic-ularly wheat, but patent activity in cotton was negligible. The technical difficulties of mechanizing the cotton harvest are undoubtedly more severe than for wheat and corn, but the patent figures presumably reflect inventive efforts rather than successes. This is not to say that cotton-growers were lethargic or that they should have behaved differently. In terms of the model of chapter 3, the observed pattern is

39. Easterlin, "Farm Production and Income," p. 95.
40. Gallman, "The Agricultural Sector." On the geographical problems of non-cotton agriculture in the Deep South, see Julius Rubin, "The Limits of Agricultural Progress in the Nineteenth-Century South."
41. These patent figures were first brought to bear on these issues by Jay Mandle, in an unpublished paper presented at the September, 1974, Rochester conference on *Time on the Cross*.

TABLE 4.1.
Patents Granted per Year for Mechanical Devices for Grain and Corn Harvesting, Threshing, and Cutting, and for Cotton Harvesting, Picking, and Chopping

	CORN	GRAIN	COTTON
1837–1849	3.5	6.5	0.2
1850–1860	18.5	10.5	2.6
1866–1879	39.3	38.5	13.2
1880–1890	44.2	59.5	30.5
1891–1900	53.9	56.0	22.9
1901–1914	69.1	52.2	53.6

SOURCE: Jacob Schmookler, *Patents, Inventions, and Economic Change* (Cambridge: Harvard University Press, 1972), pp. 100–103.

perfectly understandable: during a period of rapid demand expansion, Northern farmers increasingly pressed against labor constraints and searched for mechanical means of increasing acreage and output.[42] In the South, in contrast, it was sensible for planters to concentrate on geographical expansion, systems of labor management, and (for somewhat different reasons) the political security of slave property. In support of this interpretation—that the antebellum patent figures reflect the internal logic of slavery and family farms, not inherent features of the crops or Southern backwardness in inventiveness or culture—note that the Southern figures jump sharply upward after emancipation, and that during the next period of acceleration in cotton demand (1900–1914) cotton is a near match for the other two crops.

The significance of slower mechanization in cotton does not, therefore, have to do with the rate of agricultural progress, but with the implications for the emergence of nonagricultural economic activity. In the northwestern states, the agricultural implements industry was one of the

42. This is one way of interpreting the argument of Paul A. David in "The Mechanization of Reaping in the Ante-Bellum Midwest."

largest and most dynamic components of mid-century manufacturing, in emerging cities like Chicago and in countless
smaller towns producing for farmers in the surrounding
areas.[43] In the South this activity was largely absent: during
the great cotton surge of the 1850s, the value of agricultural implements produced declined absolutely in the states
of the Deep South.[44]

This is only one of several effects by which the internal
logic of slavery slowed the growth of nonagricultural economic activity in the South. The whole discussion of agricultural progress would be much less important if the region
had developed other strong economic sectors into which
resources could have shifted during periods of slack cotton
demand. A complete discussion of this topic is beyond the
scope of this book, but a number of critical considerations
flow directly from the framework laid out thus far.

That the South was behind the rest of the nation in
nonagricultural economic activity has never been in dispute: a few indicators of relative backwardness in manufacturing and in the growth of cities—two variables that
are by no means equivalent in the antebellum period, but
which reflect two different dimensions of the same general
subject—may be found in Tables 4 2 and 4.3. Several economists have interpreted this evidence to mean only that "the
South's lag behind the North in industrialization is fully consistent with the proposition that during the antebellum
era the South's comparative advantage was in agriculture
rather than in manufacturing." [45] This perspective views
each region as "responding to existing factor endowments
and specializing according to these differences" in the manner

43. David, "Mechanization of Reaping," pp. 3–6.
44. U.S. Bureau of the Census, Eighth Census of the United States
(1860), *Manufacturing*, p. ccxvii. The very drastic decline reported for
the state of Georgia may be in error, but the figures leave no doubt
about the regional contrast.
45. Fogel and Engerman, *Time on the Cross*, 1:255. Conrad and
Meyer state a similar view: "Economic considerations or (if you wish)
profit-seeking are also quite sufficient to explain the South's concentration upon agricultural development," "Slavery as an Obstacle to Economic Growth," p. 528.

TABLE 4.2.

REGIONAL PATTERNS OF MANUFACTURING

	Capital Invested by Manufacturing per Capita		Value of Manufacturing Output per Capita	
	1850	1860	1850	1860
New England	$57.96	$82.13	$100.71	$149.47
Middle States	35.50	52.21	71.24	96.28
Northwest	11.70	18.95	26.32	37.33
Pacific States	10.39	42.35	84.83	129.04
South	7.60	10.54	10.88	17.09
Cotton South	5.11	7.20	6.83	10.47
U.S.	22.73	32.12	43.69	59.98

SOURCES: U.S. Bureau of the Census, *Compendium of 1850 Census*, p. 179; Eighth U.S. Census, *Manufactures*, p. 725; Ninth Census, *Compendium*, p. 799.

TABLE 4.3.

REGIONAL PATTERNS OF URBANIZATION
(BY PERCENT OF POPULATION)

	1820	1830	1840	1850	1860
New England	10.5	14.0	19.4	28.8	36.6
Middle Atlantic	11.3	14.2	18.1	25.5	35.4
East North Central	1.2	2.5	3.9	9.0	14.1
West North Central	....	3.5	3.9	10.3	13.4
South Atlantic	5.5	6.2	7.7	9.8	11.5
East South Central	0.8	1.5	2.1	4.2	5.9

SOURCE: North, *Economic Growth*, p. 258.

classically described by international trade theory.[46] This simple argument has been powerful and difficult to refute. Critics have generally been forced to argue in somewhat vague terms that slave labor was not well-suited to non-agricultural work, that patterns of demand generated by

46. Fred Bateman and Thomas Weiss, "Comparative Regional Development in Antebellum Manufacturing," p. 183. Cf. Lee Benson's statement: ". . . the relatively low rates of industrialization and urbanization in the South prior to 1861 were rational, fully in line with

slavery did not mesh well with antebellum manufacturing technology, or that the "distinct politics, ideology, and pattern of social behavior" of plantation slavery was hostile to industrial development—arguments that are at best difficult to define precisely and verify, at worst easily refuted.[47] Without suggesting dismissal of any of these hypotheses on which research is still in progress, the model of chapter 3 suggests a simpler argument.

The secret of getting the right answer lies in posing the question properly. The fallacy in the analysis just presented is not in the claim that Southern resources were allocated according to the principle of comparative advantage, but in the implicit assumption that the North developed a thriving manufacturing sector because the North had a comparative advantage in manufacturing. The problem is once again the tyranny of words, in this case one of the most misused terms in the economic vocabulary. As frequently used, the term comparative advantage is no more than a tautology: goods would not be produced unless it were profitable to do so, and if it was profitable to produce these goods, the region must have had a comparative advantage in those

---

classical capitalist economic theory" ("Explanations of American Civil War Causation," p. 258). The Fogel-Engerman argument that slavery possessed a special productivity advantage in staple-crop production presumably implies a shift in Southern comparative advantage away from manufacturing. But such an argument is quite different from the one advanced here. We also omit discussion of the theoretical possibility that an extremely low demand elasticity for cotton might reverse the net affect of such a bias in balanced-trade general equilibrium.

47. The quotation is from Eugene D. Genovese, *The Political Economy of Slavery*, p. 157, in a chapter ("The Significance of the Slave Plantation for Southern Economic Development," published originally in *Journal of Southern History* 28 [November 1962]) that actually stresses the weakness of market demand. The imprecision of this argument is attacked by Robert Fogel, "The Specification Problem in Economic History," *Journal of Economic History* 27 (September 1967), pp. 285–89. A restatement, with empirical evidence, is provided by William N. Parker, "Slavery and Southern Economic Development," but the empirical conclusions are questioned in Bateman and Weiss, pp. 190–94.

The argument that slaves cannot be used effectively in manufacturing goes back to John E. Cairnes, *The Slave Power*, pp. 70–73 and Ulrich B. Phillips, "The Economic Cost of Slaveholding in the Cotton

goods. If economists can speak so loosely, then the parrot who became an economist by learning to say "supply and demand" will become an international economist by learning only one more term. If the concept is to have substantive historical content, it must be taken instead as a refutable hypothesis to the effect that regional specialization is determined by relative costs of production, which in turn result from factors inherent in each region's endowment of productive resources—where the term "resource" can be defined broadly so as to include qualitative categories like "skilled labor," but where we can reasonably reject as verging on tautology such "resources" as "knowledge," "ideology," or "entrepreneurial energy." One might reasonably insist as well on distinguishing the effects of resource endowments from those of institutions such as slavery or family farms. Within the bounds of a restrictive definition such as this, it has never been shown that a comparative advantage in manufacturing was a necessary condition for successful nineteenth-century industrialization, and the clearest historical counterexample is the American North.

Until at least the 1820s and probably later, many contemporary observers believed that the factor endowment of the United States could never support a large manufacturing sector. Their reasoning was not very different from a simple comparative advantage argument that, because of the abundance of land, the high productivity of labor in American agriculture would keep wages too high for manufacturing to compete successfully internationally.[48] Frequently, a roughly equivalent point was stated as a principle of behavior on the part of family farmers, which would inhibit the

---

Belt," but numerous counterexamples are provided in Robert S. Starobin, *Industrial Slavery in the Old South.*

Generalized arguments about the antagonisms between planters and industrial-urban development are frequently found—for example, Genovese, *Political Economy*, chaps. 8–9, and Richard C. Wade, *Slavery in the Cities*—but it usually remains unclear what mechanism thwarts the economic incentives involved.

48. See Frederick W. Taussig, *The Tariff History of the United States* (New York: Capricorn Books, 1964; first published, 1892), p. 65.

development of a wage labor supply. Benjamin Franklin wrote in 1760:

> But no man, who can have a piece of land of his own, sufficient by his labor to subsist his family in plenty, is poor enough to be a manufacturer, and work for a master. Hence, when there is land enough in America for our people, there can never be manufacturers to any amount of value.[49]

One of the major tasks of nineteenth-century American economic history is explaining why these straightforward predictions, consistent with basic economic principles, did not prove correct. A full discussion of the topic would take us far afield, but even a partial list of relevant considerations would have to include the following: (a) that creative entrepreneurial and technological energies developed a uniquely American manufacturing technology and organization, which substituted for scarce factors and made use of abundant natural resources like timber;[50] (b) that the character of agricultural progress involved important linkages to local industrialization;[51] (c) that scarce inputs, especially investment capital and immigrant labor, were available from outside the region, allowing industrial expansion to proceed

49. Quoted in Alexander Field, "Educational Reform and Manufacturing Development in Mid-Nineteenth Century Massachusetts," p. 189.

50. H. S. Habbakuk, *American and British Technologies in the Nineteenth Century* (Cambridge: At the University Press, 1967); E. Ames and N. Rosenberg, "The Enfield Arsenal in Theory and History," *Economic Journal* (December 1968). The most recent formulation of the "Habbakuk hypothesis" is in Paul A. David, *Technical Choice, Innovation and Economic Growth* (New York: Cambridge University Press, 1975), chap. 1, but the theoretical issues debated there are not really critical to the present discussion.

51. David, "Mechanization of Reaping," pp. 3–9; Albert Fishlow, *American Railroads and the Transformation of the Ante-Bellum Economy* (Cambridge: Harvard University Press, 1965), chaps. 4, 8 and, *a fortiori*, the rest of the book; Louis C. Hunter, "Influence of the Market upon Technique in the Iron Industry in Western Pennsylvania up to 1860," *Journal of Economic and Business History* 1 (February 1929), esp. pp. 241, 266–72. As in n. 51 above, the point made here is essentially independent of the issue raised by Peter Temin in "A New Look at Hunter's Hypothesis about the Ante-bellum Iron Industry," *American Economic Review* 54 (May 1964).

in a fashion not governed by regional resource endowments.[52] On each of these counts, the internal logic of slavery was altogether different.

(a) *Entrepreneurship.* Following Fleisig, we understand the concept of entrepreneurship to involve the ability to make unusual absolute amounts of money using commonly available productive resources. These skills are not easily measurable, but we assume that they are possessed by only a fraction of the population, and for the sake of argument we assume that there is no difference between North and South in entrepreneurial talent. As argued in chapter 3, the crucial distinction between slavery and family-farm agriculture was that slavery removed the major obstacle to farm expansion and hence to the accumulation of a large absolute fortune within agriculture. Thus, one need not argue that slavery biased the allocation of entrepreneurship against manufacturing in relation to market-determined profit-abilities; it was family farming that biased entrepreneurship against agriculture, by greatly limiting the opportunities for expansion of scale. In the slave South an entrepreneur could achieve and expand and use productively a large personal fortune within the agricultural sector. Surely it is this effect that writers are reaching for in accusing planters of "inertia" in their investment patterns. The point that is missed is that the absence of such inertia in the North is readily explained by the fact that no entrepreneur had open to him the option that the planters accepted!

One simple version of the argument is diagrammed in Figure 4.4, adapted from Fleisig, which shows the distribution of entrepreneurs between sectors as a function of absolute returns. The diagram assumes that returns in each sector are a declining function of the number of entrepreneurs in that sector (read industry from left to right, agriculture from right to left), and that entrepreneurs move so as to equalize the marginal absolute returns in the two

52. The importance of capital inflows in the 1830s and labor inflows thereafter is shown in Douglass C. North, *The Economic Growth of the United States, 1790–1860,* esp. chap. 9 and pp. 71, 194, 197–98, 206–7, 211.

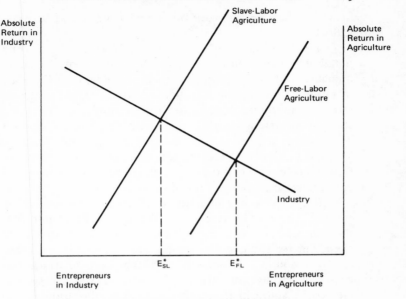

FIGURE 4.4. *Absolute Returns and the Distribution of Entrepreneurs Between Agriculture and Industry*

NOTE: Horizontal distance is total number of entrepreneurs. E^*_{FL} is distribution of entrepreneurs in free-labor system; E^*_{SL} in slave system.

sectors. Slavery, by opening up opportunities in agriculture, shifts the distribution (E^*_{SL}) toward that sector compared to the free-labor point (E^*_{FL}): but one could just as easily regard the slave-labor curve as the norm and the free-labor curve as biased, i.e., the one for which opportunities in agriculture were closed off. It is difficult to confirm this analysis in any direct empirical way, but the entrepreneural model is obviously consistent with the evidence on agricultural wealth distributions presented in chapter 2, and it is also consistent with the further evidence (cited there) that region-wide wealth distributions including cities and industry do not differ greatly North and South. Conversely, the profitability calculations of Bateman, Foust, and Weiss have shown just how far from reality is an alternative model in which the rate of return on capital is equalized between sectors.[53]

There was one kind of activity in Northern agriculture that held some promise of large absolute returns to entrepreneurs: land speculation.[54] We do not intend in the least to minimize the importance of land speculation. Its greater relative importance in the North was a direct result of the contrast in systems of property, in which the accumulation of wealth in the form of capitalized labor was not possible. We argue below that the incentives resulting from this contrast marked another decisive difference in developmental patterns between the two regions.

(b) *Agricultural Demands.* This effect has been largely covered earlier. The essence of the argument is not that slave agriculture was unmechanized because it was inefficient, but for the opposite reason that the system of "labor as a commodity" promoted a very high degree of static efficiency in resource allocation. Conversely, it was the tension created by static inefficiencies in resource allocation in the North (the pressing of farms against microeconomic labor constraints) that generated the early impulse to mechanization. This development not only gave the North an early start toward a modern agricultural technology, but in turn gave

53. Fred Bateman, James Foust, and Thomas Weiss, "Profitability in Southern Manufacturing," esp. pp. 220, 226. Beyond this rather negative inference, this careful study is unfortunately of limited relevance for our concerns. The authors are unable, due to the limitations of their data, to distinguish free from slave labor, and capital invested in slaves from investment in plant, equipment, etc. For the same reason, they neglect capital gains on slave property. Hence the meaning of their evidence is most obscure on the very points raised here, particularly since there is evidence that profitability on Northern manufactures (similarly calculated) was also high.

54. The term "land speculation" has such diverse connotations that it would be best avoided were it not so commonly used in the nineteenth century. It frequently refers only to the holding of land in large units for no productive purpose. As used here, however, speculation has a much broader reference to economic activity that is influenced by expectations of future land price increases. Similarly, speculation in slave values often refers to the purchase of slaves solely for resale, but it is used much more broadly here. In both cases, however, our emphasis is not on the notion of speculative *holding* of these assets, but on the incentives to engage in property-value augmenting activity.

rise to a widely diffused agricultural implements industry, which had close links to the early iron and coal industries.[55] What we observe throughout the North is not an expansion of agriculture at the absolute expense of manufacturing, but a mutual growth and a fruitful interaction between sectors at a local level.[56] Table 4.2 shows that even the most agricultural of Northern regions had higher levels of manufacturing output than the South.

These developments were accelerated by the phenomenon of land speculation, universal in the North but rendered less important in the South by the possibility of accumulating and speculating in slave property. Speculative motives encouraged farmers to hold larger acreages than their families could farm, which in turn increased the potential benefits from mechanization. In addition, the expectant interest in land values generated in the North a strong political demand for internal improvements—canals, highways, local marketing facilities, public education, and railroads.[57] For small- and medium-scale farmers, land speculation was virtually the only possibility for major capital gains in the North; in the South, not only was another form of property available, but it was a form of property whose value was completely independent of local development. As Edward Ruffin put it in 1859, "slaves, being movable, will be rated in price, not by their profits in their actual location, but according to their profits in any other region to which they can be easily transferred." [58]

(c) *Industrial Labor Supply.* The mobility of slaves, the

55. See references in n. 51 above.

56. Clarence Danhof cites an 1850 estimate that "at least 200 different patterns of plows" were being manufactured in the North (*Change in Agriculture,* p. 192).

57. On railroads and farmers, see Fishlow, chap. 4. For a more general argument about the pervasive influence of land speculation, see Leslie E. Decker, "The Great Speculation: An Interpretation of Mid-Continent Pioneering." Benson (pp. 258–63) also stresses land speculation, but limits his discussion of slavery to its effects on augmenting land values, overlooking the much larger speculation in slave values themselves.

58. Edmund Ruffin, "The Effects of High Prices of Slaves," *De-Bow's Review* 26 (June 1859): 648.

existence under slavery of a reasonably efficient region-wide market in capitalized labor, is also the key to slavery's inhibiting influence on the development of an industrial labor force. This inhibiting effect does not reflect institutional rigidity or inefficiency on the part of slavery, nor, necessarily, distaste for the use of slaves in manufacturing. But it was the absence of such an efficient Northern labor market that allowed, contrary to Benjamin Franklin, the emergence of a native-born factory-labor force in New England in the 1820s, 1830s, and 1840s. Labor for these factories was generated indirectly by the opening of the West to commercial agriculture during this period, as New England farm families found themselves undercut by the new inflow of cheap foodstuffs. The efficient national resource allocation, in terms of resource endowments, was for New England farmers to move in large numbers to the better land in the West. They did so in large numbers, but because these moves had to be desired, planned, and financed through thousands of microlevel decisions, there were many who were left behind—because they were ignorant, because they lacked funds, or because they were women. This group provided the labor for early factories, at wages which did not reflect the value of their hypothetical productivity in western farming.[59]

One might, after all, object to some of the earlier discussion by arguing that it was not the North that had a comparative advantage in manufacturing, but the Northeast, or perhaps New England. But this objection only solidifies the point: the concept of comparative advantage can apply only if we can identify an economic region, an identification that implies only limited possibilities for the movement of factors of production between regions. New England was, loosely speaking, a region by this definition, and it is true enough that the rise of manufacturing was encouraged by

59. This account draws heavily on Field, chap. 7. Field argues that young women were increasingly available for factory work because of the exodus of young men. See also Field, "Sectoral Shift in Antebellum Massachusetts: A Reconsideration" [*Explorations in Economic History* 15 (April 1978)].

the relative infertility of New England farmland, as the theory of comparative advantage asserts. But why not say the same of the Southeast, which had a very similar agricultural history of early settlement on land of well below average fertility? One essential reason is the unified slave labor market: any slaveowner who lacked the knowledge, energy, or funds to move west had only to sell his slaves. He would get full value, for Southeastern slaves (male and female) were priced according to their productivity in Southwestern cotton farming: there were no bargains for prospective employers of slaves in manufacturing.

There are two possible loopholes in this analysis: first, one might argue that the location behavior of immigrant labor was the more important factor, since the foreign-born were increasingly prominent in Northern manufacturing after the early 1840s; second, one might ask why Southern manufacturers were not able to develop successfully using free white labor during the prewar period. With respect to the first point, one should not underplay the importance of New England's early start using native-born labor, since her position of technological leadership carried important momentum to the rest of the economy.[60] The locational choices of immigrant workers were surely affected by these pre-potato-famine patterns. With respect to the second point, it is true that the beginnings of a potential white factory labor force in the Southeast can be seen before 1860, and that by that year unskilled slave labor in factories had been largely displaced.[61] The comparative lateness of this development may be attributed to the fact that the small

60. As described in Nathan Rosenberg, "Technological Change in the Machine Tool Industry, 1840–1910," *Journal of Economic History* 23 (December 1963). The importance of "learning" effects in New England textiles is stressed in David, "Learning by Doing and Tariff Protection," *Journal of Economic History* 30 (December 1970), reprinted in *Technical Choice.*

61. Tom E. Terrill, "Eager Hands: Labor for Southern Textiles, 1850–1860," *Journal of Economic History* 36 (March 1976); Diffee W. Standard and Richard W. Griffen, "The Cotton Textile Industry in Antebellum North Carolina," *North Carolina Historical Review* 34 (January–April 1957); Ernest M. Lander, *The Textile Industry in Antebellum South Carolina* (Baton Rouge: Louisiana State University Press, 1969), pp. 90–91.

free farmers of the Southeast were much less involved in production of food crops for the market, and hence were less easily displaced by Western foodstuffs; the counterparts of the commercialized New England farmers (in this sense only) were the slaves, who were rarely used in factories for the reasons suggested. Also, the opening of the Southwest did not actually bring an antebellum fall in the cotton price, because demand was so strong. Thus, resource endowments and world demand were clearly involved: but note that the absence of extensive commercial food growing in the Southeast was also a result of the limited development of cities and towns in that region; and that Southeastern manufacturers in the 1850s could have used the same labor source as their Northeastern competitors—immigrants—if they could have attracted some.

The essential point about each of these arguments is this: it does not make sense to attribute Southern industrial backwardness to factor endowments or to immigrant behavior *instead* of to slavery, unless it can be shown that patterns of immigration were independent of the existence of slavery. The economists who have analyzed antebellum development have assumed this independence: sometimes explicitly, but then primarily with reference to moral objections to slavery on the part of immigrants; [62] more often implicitly, by concentration on *per capita* figures and assuming that *per capita* development is not affected by population growth.[63] But it is completely unreasonable to assert that land-labor relationships, comparative advantage, and urbanization are independent of inflows of labor. In the next section we argue that on economic grounds it is equally unreasonable to assert that inflows of free labor were unaffected by the presence of slavery in the South.

62. William L. Miller, "Slavery and the Population of the South." See also Benson, pp. 293–94.
63. Stanley Engerman, "A Reconsideration of Southern Economic Growth, 1770–1860"; Engerman, "Some Economic Factors in Southern Backwardness in the Nineteenth Century," in *Essays in Regional Economics*, eds. John F. Kain and John R. Meyer (Cambridge: Harvard University Press, 1971).

Slavery, Immigration, and the Cities

One of the most influential recent works arguing the incompatibility of slavery and modern urban-industrial development has been Richard Wade's *Slavery in the Cities: The South 1820–1860*.[64] Wade documents extensively the dangers, fears, and hostilities toward the existence of a large urban slave population. He clinches his case by showing that the slave population in most Southern cities had declined, relatively from at least 1830, and absolutely during the 1850s.[65] However, another recent book, by Claudia Goldin, shows econometrically that the demand for slaves in most cities was in fact rising during the 1850s; slaves were pulled out of these cities by strong agricultural demand, not pushed out by increasing disruption and fear. The underlying reason for the sensitivity of urban slavery to demand fluctuations is, according to her estimates, that the urban demand for slaves was much more elastic (price sensitive) than the rural demand.[66] The argument can be understood using Figure 4.4, replacing "entrepreneurs" by "slave labor," and viewing the curves as urban and rural demand curves for slave labor: the curves are drawn so that urban demand has a much higher elasticity. Fluctuations in urban demand will have very little effect on the allocation of slaves; relatively small fluctuations in the inelastic rural demand, however, will have a major impact on the number of slaves in cities.

Claudia Goldin's results are completely consistent with the argument of this book, but her interpretation of the evidence differs at several points. First, Goldin accepts the Fogel-Engerman explanation for the difference in elasticities, namely that "the slave form of labor enabled scale economies to be achieved in agriculture which were not possible with free labor," whereas, "there were no great economies in employing slave labor in urban industry." [67] It has

64. New York: Oxford University Press, 1964.
65. *Ibid.*, pp. 325–30.
66. *Urban Slavery in the American South 1820–1860.*
67. *Ibid.*, pp. 105, 125.

never been clear why the organizational productivity gains from division of labor under slavery should have been so great in agriculture, yet nonexistent in the very factories that inspired this concept. But if instead, as argued here, these "economies of scale" were actually only a transfer of labor from non-market to market activity, then it is no surprise to learn that there is no further productivity advantage in relation to wage laborers whose output is completely monetized. This same consideration points to one kind of economic bias against the use of slaves in urban areas, in no way refuted by Goldin's work: the opportunity to reduce risk by vertical integration (primarily providing the food supply from on-farm production) is no longer present in urban areas. Because the subsistence needs of the slave must be provided for no matter how business is going, an investor with limited personal wealth would find that the risk of loss of his own capital is greater because of the larger cash outlay required—even if the expected yield on the investment in the slave is equivalent to that in agriculture.[68]

A more important difference in interpretation concerns the relationship between urban slavery and the immigration of free wage laborers into Southern cities. Goldin treats the level of such immigration as an exogenous variable, i.e., determined independently of the rest of her model. Yet her empirical work shows not only that urban slavery was sensitive to slave price changes, but that an influx of free laborers led directly to an exodus of slaves; at some points the relative absence of immigrants is taken as an exogenous explanation for the level of the elasticity itself.[69] But if we reverse the

68. If Ps is the investment in the slave, the standard deviation of the return on his personal capital (C) will be

$$\frac{Ps + M}{C} Se$$

where M is the required (cash) maintenance expenditures, and Se is the standard deviation of the return on the entire investment. The absence of such vertical integration is in fact noted by Goldin (p. 105). The existence of a "bias" against the use of slave labor in cities is not refuted by Goldin because her evidence relates to changes in urban slavery over time, not to the average level over the whole period.

69. *Ibid.*, pp. 97–98, 114.

question, could we ask for better evidence that the immigration of free labor into Southern cities was sensitive to the presence of slaves? [70]

The assumption that rates of immigration were independent of slavery is all the more doubtful in light of the evidence, very ably presented by Goldin, that much of the objection to the presence of slaves in cities originated with white artisans, tradesmen, and even unskilled workers, who stood to lose economically from the presence of close substitutes. It was not just that the presence of slave substitutes tended to depress wages, but that "the use of slaves as strike breakers was common in Southern towns," an occurrence that accentuated "divisions between the white propertied and nonpropertied classes." [71] The point here is not that urban antislavery was an important force in regional politics, only that the question of slave competition was a major concern to the urban working class, small as it was. Can we review these histories and still believe that the low level of immigration into Southern cities had nothing to do with slavery? In fact, even the most successful Southern manufacturers had to recruit labor vigorously in the North, and found the presence of slaves in the labor force made such hiring especially difficult.[72]

Most of this discussion concerns the preferences of immigrants for locating in North or South. But there were also important differences in the political economy of the demand side of immigration, i.e., the structure of interests and incentives inherent in the system of propertyholding. For example, employers in the North were no less eager to

70. The assertion that "the very large oscillations in slave labor quantities experienced in the Border State cities can be explained . . . by economic factors bearing on the substitutability of slave for free labor" (p. 113) is little more than an assumption. The fundamental ambiguity of the evidence may be seen in the sentence which follows: "The loss of slave labor which many Southern cities experienced during the 1850s seems less the result of strong antislave forces in the cities than the consequence of an increased free population which was a substitute for male slave labor."

71. *Ibid.*, pp. 28–33.

72. See the account in Charles B. Dew, *Ironmaker to the Confederacy* (New Haven: Yale University Press, 1966), pp. 28–31.

break strikes and labor organizations, but one of their most common methods was to bring in immigrant strikebreakers.[73] For this function, slaves and immigrants were direct substitutes.

A regional contrast of broader significance in the antebellum era is the relationship between immigration and property values. A region of land speculators will be a region that recruits immigrant labor. A region wealthy in high-priced slaves will not. This elementary difference in vested interests, a direct function of the difference in labor systems, produced pervasive differences in public and private behavior with respect to immigration. All over the North there were people who stood to gain from immigration, from the small-scale operators and town builders to big landowners and railroads. The effects of these incentives are ultimately related to the rise of cities and towns in agricultural areas. As Decker describes the scene: [74]

> The primary means by which the little operators sought to attract the settlers necessary to force up the value of the lands they owned or claimed was to use the borrowing power of precinct and county governments to finance as many desirable public improvements (schools, roads, bridges) and to attract as many desirable services (railroads, commercial centers) as possible to the land's vicinity. Thus it was that schools with capacities far in excess of the need were immediately built, that county and precinct bonds for railroads and related promotions were voted by the firstcomers, that local debts mounted sharply during the first surge into any area.

By way of contrast there is Taylor's observation that "The scattered towns of South Carolina were somnolent, easy-

73. Charlotte Erickson, *American Industry and the European Immigrant 1860–1885* (Cambridge: Harvard University Press, 1957).

74. Decker, p. 378.

75. Rosser H. Taylor, *Antebellum South Carolina* (Chapel Hill: University of North Carolina Press, 1942), p. 81.

going market and government towns." [75] Is it really so clear that these different politics resulted from differences in attitudes toward democracy or government or the value of education, and not from basic differences in how many people stood to gain from local development and immigration? [76]

The slaveholders of the South, large and small, had little to gain from encouraging local development and immigration: most of them were no keener on free labor immigration than on allowing new slave imports. Nothing prevented land speculation and town building, but the proportional impact on wealth was much less, because the bulk of wealth was held in a form that was unaffected by local development and little affected—not positively, anyway—by immigration. Prospective employers in towns and cities of course wanted immigrants, but for the slaveholders in these communities free labor immigration just meant more trouble, if it did not indeed constitute an active threat. Finally, at the regional level, which is where their property interest directed their attention, slaveowners had reason to fear the implications of greater free labor immigration: in part because any increase in Southern labor might lower slave property values, but more importantly because a growing class of nonslaveholders, especially outsiders with non-Southern backgrounds, might create a political threat to slavery in the South, or weaken the region's strength and unity in national politics, thereby endangering the security of slave property. Thus, because of slavery, the South had no unified private or social interest in encouraging immigration. Can we reasonably believe that the actual pattern of immigration was independent of this fact?

76. Stanley Elkins and Eric McKitrick, in "A Meaning for Turner's Frontier," document the truly staggering North-South differences in numbers of small towns (pp. 341–42) and the contrast in internal improvement activity (pp. 347–48). But they overlook the basic difference in the structure of incentives in the two regions, criticizing the South for a "substance-less" politics that lacked "concrete class interest" (pp. 579–80). They forget that slaveholders formed a majority or a large minority in the states they cover (Alabama and Mississippi), and the logic of their "concrete class interest" led them to an intense concern with national rather than local politics.

Conclusion

The first half of this chapter has argued that agricultural choices in the Cotton South were limited, and that fluctuations in the rate of growth resulted primarily from changes in cotton demand. The second half has argued that slavery reduced agriculture's derived stimulus to nonagricultural economic development, as found in the North, reduced the incentive for entrepreneurial activity in manufacturing and in local development, and inhibited the formation of an industrial labor force from either native-born or foreign-born sources. These contrasts derive not from inefficiency in the slave economy, but from the absence of the creative tensions produced by static inefficiencies in the North.[77] The repercussions of this analysis are numerous. One of the least of these repercussions is the fact that per capita incomes in the South were somewhat below antebellum Northern levels, an inequality traceable to the weakness of manufacturing growth in the Southeast.[78] The overall antebellum difference by this measure is not great, the industrial gap being largely made up by agriculture, in which the South compares favorably. More significantly, the underdevelopment of urban and industrial sectors made the region dependent on cotton demand for its economic progress, and made the transition out of agriculture much slower and more difficult than it would have been with an earlier start. By the time textiles came to the South, it was a low-wage, low-skill activity using machinery built elsewhere. The growth of Southern cities only began to accelerate after 1880,[79] and analysts of the postbellum economy have found that this late urbanization had significant retarding effects on innovation and manufacturing development.[80]

77. As classically portrayed in Albert O. Hirschman, *The Strategy of Economic Development* (New Haven: Yale University Press, 1958).
78. This is evident in Easterlin's regional income estimates, as revised in Fogel and Engerman, "The Economics of Slavery," pp. 334–35.
79. Kennth Weiher, "The Cotton Industry and Southern Urbanization," esp. pp. 122–24, 126–27.
80. Allan R. Pred, *The Spatial Dynamics of U.S. Urban-Industrial Growth, 1800–1914* (Cambridge, Mass.: The M.I.T. Press, 1966), chap.

A third implication of the argument is that the slave South, too, would have faced difficulties after 1860. The continuing political friction between slaveowners and free white workers served notice that a drastic reallocation of slave labor would not have gone uncontested. Goldin's relative sanguinity is based on the observation that slaveowners almost always won these skirmishes. But the need to win these battles underscores the system's internal contradiction: that the rise of a large class of free wage laborers would have posed an increasing threat to the political dominance of slaveowners. These free laborers were not at that time hostile to slavery as an institution, only to the use of slaves in certain localities and occupations: they well understood that the landless freedmen were likely to come into the cities to work for wages.[81] It is difficult to imagine that the political loyalties of these white workers would have been the same if slaves had been shifted in large numbers into cities and factories.

This is not to say that slavery could not have survived much longer, though it would have had to pay an increasing price for its survival. Perhaps a variant of a South African compromise would have been developed, where free white workers were given sufficient guarantees and privileges to secure their political loyalty to slavery. Projections of this sort will always remain conjectural. The only thing certain is that the economic and political character of the late antebellum period could not have persisted.

---

3. For most technologically progressive industries, the advantages of metropolitan centers have historically been much more important than wage levels in the location decisions of firms. See Robert Mellman, "A Reinterpretation of the Economic History of the Post-Reconstruction South, 1877–1919," chap. 7.

81. As indeed they did. See Reynolds Farley, "The Urbanization of Negroes in the United States," esp. p. 247.

5

On Making Economic Sense of Cotton, Slavery, and the Civil War

Economic interpretations of the Civil War have come and gone over the years. They appear most often nowadays in partnership with loosely defined concepts like "modernization," whose links to economic structure are rather distant and diffuse.[1] But the concerns over economic prospects and economic threats were so immediate and so prominent in the political debates of the 1850s that it is difficult to believe that the role of economics was so remote. This chapter argues that the current dissatisfaction with economic analyses of the war stems from an inappropriate conception of what an economic interpretation should be. No reasonable historical explanation should characterize individuals as motivated solely by the pursuit of economic gain. Nor is it reasonable to view the sections as though they were negotiating and fighting over aggregate economic costs and bene-

1. One gets this impression from reading Eric Foner, "The Causes of the Civil War." For an example, see Raimondo Luraghi, "The Civil War and the Modernization of American Society," *Civil War History* 18 (September 1972).

fits, because the political leadership had neither the means nor the desire to calculate and pursue such collective goals.[2] Instead, the main task of an economic interpretation should be to show how the structure of economic interests and incentives encouraged individuals to mobilize politically, and how an underlying logic of interests and coalitions led political representatives to pursue certain lines of action. This is an ambitious program, which is by no means completed here. But the analysis of chapters 3 and 4 suggests a beginning along the following lines: In both North and South, politics were heavily influenced by the interests of propertyholders. However, there were decisive differences in the processes by which property values were determined in the two regions, and in the resulting incentives for economic and political behavior. In the North, property rights in labor were prohibited, and, hence, efforts to augment property values focused on land: land clearing and improvement, promotion of canals and railroads to improve access to markets, attracting immigrants through vigorous recruitment and offers of credit, schools, roads, etc. In the South one could own slaves, and for this reason much of the same drive toward property accumulation was channeled along very different lines. In the North energies went toward raising the value of particular farms and local areas because land is not moveable; in the South there was relatively little a slaveowner could do to raise the value of individual slaves, though he could hope to accumulate slave property over time by fostering high fertility and low mortality. Slaves were moveable personal property; the value of an owner's slave property was determined not by his individual behavior and local development, but by regional slave markets and world cotton markets, and this value was essentially uniform in all parts of the slave South at any moment. As

2. This is only one of many objections one might make to such an approach, as pursued by Gerald Gunderson, "The Origin of the American Civil War," *Journal of Economic History* 34 (December 1974) and Claudia Goldin, "The Economics of Emancipation," *Journal of Economic History* 33 (March 1973).

prices rose to levels well above the costs of replacement, concern for slave property values moved mainly into the realm of regional psychology, distinctively sensitive to expectations and fears about the economic and political future. Seen in this light, Southern political behavior did make economic sense in immediate and not just in long-run terms. It will be helpful to begin with a discussion of some of the standard economic interpretations and why they are unsatisfactory.

Direct Economic Conflicts Between North and South

One historical tradition, dating back to the work of Charles and Mary Beard, draws a distinction between slavery and economic issues, treating the first as a moral issue, the second primarily as the conflict between agrarian and industrial interests.[3] It is not easy to find North-South issues on economic policy that are separable from slavery, and one suspects that Beard's emphasis on the tariff as the nub of discontent arises at least partially by default. Southern rhetoricians generally complained about the tariff and other allegedly biased federal subsidies to Northern business and shipping interests, but one must remember that those men, too, had a difficult time finding overt examples of the Northern "oppression" that they complained of so strenuously.[4] Most recent writers have simply been unwilling to believe that such issues as the tariff, banking, and internal improve-

3. Charles and Mary Beard, *The Rise of American Civilization* (New York: Macmillan Co., 1927), 1: chaps. 14–15. On this aspect of Beard's thought, see Staughton Lynd, "On Turner, Beard and Slavery."
4. For examples, see Kenneth M. Stampp, ed., *The Causes of the Civil War*, pp. 68–75; Dwight L. Dumond, ed., *Southern Editorials on Secession*, pp. 126–28, 406–9. Note that most of these arguments are not so much specific complaints about policy as general claims of exploitation by Northern business, shipping, and financial interests; complaints, in other words, that would apply as much to England as to the North. Avery Craven notes "the almost complete absence of concrete and specific cases of injury . . ." in the secession statements (*An Historian and the Civil War*, p. 151).

ments can bear the weight of explaining the bloody conflict of the 1860s. Not only was neither region unified on these matters, but each one seems to have been greatly defused and compromised by the 1850s.[5] A survey of federal legislation of sectional interest passed during that decade shows no general trend for or against either region, and something of an increase in Southern influence on Congressional committees and the Supreme Court.[6] To be sure, such economic disputes as the nullification crisis of 1832 may have contributed in a general way to the rise of regional consciousness in the South, but even for this case, Freehling has shown that slavery was lurking not far below the surface.[7]

However, there is no good reason why economic interpretations of the war should eschew the economics of slavery. There is one potential economic cause of regional conflict that continues to have a following: the claim that the slave economy depended upon continued acquisition of fresh land, and that this expansionism was on an inevitable collision course with the desires of free white Northern settlers. The doctrine that slavery had to expand or die was of course part of the rhetoric of some politicians in the 1850s; it received scholarly support from the British econ-

---

5. See particularly, Richard Hofstadter, "The Tariff Issue on the Eve of the Civil War," *American Historical Review* 44 (October 1938); Barrington Moore, "The American Civil War; Robert R. Russel, *Economic Aspects of Southern Sectionalism*, chap. 6.

In a recent article, Clayne Pope goes so far as to question whether it was actually true that the South stood to lose from the tariff, in light of the inelastic world demand for U.S. cotton. While theoretically interesting, this argument is probably only an intellectual curiosity. It would be compelling only in a "barter" world of balanced international trade, and in any case, Pope's own best estimates (which employ a demand elasticity that is probably too low) and independent empirical evidence suggest that the orthodox assumption that the tariff hurt cotton growers is appropriate. See Clayne Pope, "The Impact of the Ante-Bellum Tariff on Income Distribution," *Explorations in Economic History* 9 (Summer 1972); Bennett D. Baack and Edward Ray, "Tariff Policy and Income Distribution: The Case of the U.S. 1830–1860," *Explorations in Economic History* 11 (Winter 1973–74).

6. Dean Yarwood, "A Failure in Coalition Maintenance, pp. 227–30.

7. William W. Freehling, *Prelude to Civil War*.

omist J. E. Cairnes,[8] and in recent times has been defended by such dissimilar writers as Eugene Genovese and the economists Conrad and Meyer.[9] This is a tempting hypothesis on several counts, among which is that it seems to flow naturally from the very definition of slavery as capitalized labor. Whereas in the free labor economy of the North, westward expansion threatened to hurt eastern business by driving up the wages of labor, in the South planters were in a position to capture the benefits of more expensive labor, in the form of higher slave prices. Thus, the North was economically of two minds about territorial expansion, but the South had an interest in expansion that unified east and west.

The problem with this logically sound argument is that it just doesn't work. Whatever the importance of expansion to slaveholders, there is no evidence to indicate that they were "feeling the pinch" of land shortage in the 1850s.[10] Supplies of untouched cotton land were vast within the 1860 boundaries of the slave states, as Cairnes himself recognized: "For nearly a quarter of a century—ever since the annexation of Texas—the territory at the disposal of the South has been much greater than its available slave force has been able to cultivate; and its most urgent need has now

8. *The Slave Power*, esp. chaps. 1–2, 4, 6.
9. Alfred Conrad and John R. Meyer wrote: "Continued expansion of slave territory was both possible and, to some extent, necessary. The maintenance of profits in the Old South depended upon the expansion, extensive or intensive, of slave agriculture into the Southwest. This is sufficient to explain the interest of the Old South in secession and does away with the necessity to fall back upon arguments of statemanship or quixotism to explain the willingness to fight for the peculiar institution." ("The Economics of Slavery in the Antebellum South," p. 121). Eugene D. Genovese's view is remarkably similar: "The sale of surplus slaves depended on markets further south, which necessarily depended on virgin lands on which to apply the old, wasteful methods of farming. . . . The steady acquisition of new land could alone guarantee the maintenance of that interregional slave trade which held the system together." (*The Political Economy of Slavery*, p. 247.) A more recent but less precise formulation of the argument may be found in William L. Barney, *The Secessionist Impulse*, pp. 3–26.
10. Barney, p. 8.

become, not more virgin soils on which to employ its slaves, but more slaves for the cultivation of its virgin soils." [11] If we ask what microeconomic pressures might have been generated by land shortage, we find that, in fact, improved acreage was growing more rapidly than population in every cotton state; the rise in land values reflected these ongoing improvements and the prosperity of the cotton boom— only the relatively small fraction of the population that owned no land before the boom could view this rising wealth as an economic squeeze in any objective sense. And in light of the evidence of rising average land values, can we reasonably believe that Southerners were politically agitated over soil exhaustion in the midst of the spectacular cotton yields of the late 1850s? [12]

In short, the land-expansion hypothesis as argued by Cairnes and his followers is an economic *Hamlet* without the prince. At most, it could explain the emergence of sectional conflict over a much longer time period, but not the intensification of these conflicts during the 1850s. Even for the longer period, it is not clear that slaveholders on balance stood to gain from a more rapid westward expansion of Southern agriculture, because of the unique place of American cotton in the world markets. Any slaveowner could find a buyer for his slaves if he chose to; the relevant question is whether westward expansion tended, as Cairnes believed, to raise the price of slaves.[13] For this calculation, one has to set the effects of additional land on productivity against the effects of additional cotton on the cotton price. One simulation experiment estimates the positive elasticity at .32 (percentage change in output/percentage change in land), the negative elasticity between −.439 and −.495 dur-

11. Cairnes, p. 202. See also Lewis Cecil Gray, *History of Agriculture in the Southern United States to 1860*, pp. 641–42; Robert W. Fogel and Stanley L. Engerman calculated that the acreage in cotton nearly doubled between 1860 and 1890 ("The Economics of Slavery," p. 331).
12. Barney, pp. 11–15.
13. Cairnes, pp. 125–26. Note that the South's major act of expansion was seen by Cairnes as the Louisiana Purchase.

ing the period 1830 to 1860.[14] Such a calculation can only be the roughest approximation to the actual net effects, but when one recalls that it neglects entirely any effects on southeastern land values or free labor supplies, it becomes still more difficult to maintain that the South had reason to be any more unified on expansion than the North.

Now one may argue that these economic effects were not all equally visible at the time, but the effects of policies on the price of cotton were certainly not outside the attention of planters. For example, in 1829 when Senator Hayne of South Carolina delivered his first speech opposing the tariff and advocating a cheap land-sales policy, he was criticized at home on precisely these grounds, for "supporting a measure infinitely more destructive [than the tariff] to the interests of his constituents." [15] In the 1830s and 1840s the South showed no unity on the issues of territorial expansion and the distribution of public lands. A study by Dean Yarwood of the lines of cleavage in the Congress of 1850 shows that "the question of the disposition of western lands was an entirely separate dimension" from the North-South sectional split.[16] (This was not true in 1860, by

14. Peter Passell and Gavin Wright, "The Effects of Pre-Civil War Territorial Expansion on the Price of Slaves," pp. 1191–94. In this article we show that in a simple two-factor production model, the net change in the slave price is given by

$$P_s' = \phi \; (F_s' + P_c')$$

where F_s' is the percentage change in the marginal product of slave labor, P_c' is the percentage change in the cotton price, and ϕ is the ratio of gross revenue to net revenue in the base period. The elasticity f_s'/L', where L' is the percentage change in land, is shown to be equal to the ratio a/b, where a is the share of land in total product and b is the elasticity of substitution. P_c' is estimated by simulation of an econometric model of cotton markets. The value chosen for a is in fact irrelevant to the net result, though the value chosen for b is critical. Our conclusion is supported by a more elaborate analysis in Laurence J. Kotlikoff and Sebastion E. Pinero, "The Old South's Stake in the Inter-Regional Movement of Slaves, 1850–1860."

15. Quoted in Freehling, *Prelude to Civil War*, p. 184.

16. Dean Yarwood, "Legislative Persistence: A Comparison of the U.S. Senate in 1850 and 1860."

which time the crisis had deepened to the point where the votes on almost every issue divided on sectional lines.) As late as 1854, the South divided on the Homestead Act along east-west and party lines (and according to whether or not a state had public lands within its boundaries), almost as markedly as the North.[17] Again and again the South seems not to have been united on any economic policies, even those connected with slavery, but only on the issue of slavery *qua* slavery; it was the sectional crisis over slavery that conveyed regional unity onto economic legislation and other issues.

Having found these actual economic conflicts insubstantial, many writers, including Yarwood, conclude that it must have been the apprehension of future policies on economics and slavery that led the South to secede.[18] This argument is difficult to refute, but it is rendered suspect by the fact that it often seems to be reached by precisely this process of logical elimination. It is true enough that the Republican platform of 1860 contained an economic program not altogether to Southern liking; but none of these proposals were new, and it was, after all, the South's bolting of the Democratic party in 1860 that made Lincoln's election inevitable. One can find statements reflecting all sorts of apprehensions and fears, but there is also an abundance of contradictory testimony, and unless it can be shown that these fears manifested themselves in actual behavior or pressures or incentives, or in some way reflected a perception of real trends, the argument is unconvincing.

This leaves till last the most straightforward motive, involving both economics and slavery: the North wanted to abolish slavery, and the slaveowners of the South wanted to retain their valuable property. The trouble is, while the latter is surely true, the former is not. It is not just that

17. Gerald Wolff, "The Slavocracy and the Homestead Problem of 1854."

18. Yarwood, "A Failure in Coalition Maintenance," p. 232. Yarwood reaches this conclusion virtually by deduction, after effectively demolishing claims that the South had suffered real damage or was losing power in national politics.

one is hard put to find Northerners with an economic interest in abolishing slavery.[19] Northern opinion and dominant political groups simply did not advocate such measures. Benson goes so far as to assert:

> Had Northerners held a referendum in November, 1860, solely on a proposition requiring the Federal government to require the Southern state governments to abolish slavery by some form of legislative action, probably no more than 2 per cent, almost certainly no more than 5 per cent, of the Northern electorate would have voted "Aye." [20]

The issue of abolition is of course quite different from the question of the extension of slavery into the territories, on which free farmers and miners had an economic interest buttressed by racial prejudice.[21] This basic difference between abolitionism and free-soil expansion helps to explain the popularity in the North of the rhetorical formulation that arresting the "further spread" of slavery would place the institution "in the course of ultimate extinction." It allowed Republican leaders to base a free-soil doctrine on moral hostility towards slavery, while at the same time explaining to their abolitionist constituency why they advocated no action whatsoever against slavery itself.[22]

The economic logic of the Republican political strategy of 1860 is illuminated by a recent article by Peter Passell and Maria Schmundt, which develops an essentially Beardian model of the political relations between Northeast and Northwest over the period 1820 to 1860.[23] By postulating a simple pattern of regional specialization in which eastern

19. Conversely, it is easy to find important Northern groups with an economic interest in preserving slavery. See Philip S. Foner, *Business and Slavery;* Thomas H. O'Connor, *Lords of the Loom.*

20. Lee Benson, "Explanations of American Civil War Causation," p. 246. Cf. also pp. 295–303.

21. See especially Eugene Berwanger, *The Frontier Against Slavery.*

22. This point is made in Benson, pp. 296–303.

23. Peter Passell and Maria Schmundt, "Pre–Civil War Land Policy and the Growth of Manufacturing."

capital and western land compete for the available labor supply, Passell and Schmundt show that the interests of capitalists with respect to land policy will depend on conditions of international trade and migration. If there is no foreign trade in commodities, but labor flows freely from outside, the interests of capital will actually be advanced by a cheap land policy because the improved terms of trade for manufactured goods outweigh the higher wage costs.

Thus, as immigrants increasingly took the places of native-born workers during the 1840s and 1850s, a community of economic interest began to emerge between Northeast and Northwest, and the logic of a political coalition which would put this program into effect became more and more attractive. The 1860 platform of the Republican party, and its slogans ("Vote yourself a farm," "Vote yourself a tariff") seem a perfect embodiment of the idea.[24]

There is nothing novel about the observation that the flow of people, commerce, and railroads took on an increasingly east-west character over time, and that these trends contributed to national polarization. The direction of these flows was closely related to the absence of slavery in the North, and the Passell-Schmundt model suggests some of the political repercussions on matters of economic policy. But even this very simple model—which abstracts from any number of countervailing Northern interests and opinions—gives little basis for predicting a war. There is nothing here to suggest that groups in the North had anything to gain from aggressiveness or hostility toward slavery or the South, or that the program itself embodied any important economic damage to Southern interests. There is a clear economic interest in excluding slavery from the territories, but as we have seen, this exclusion did not involve important losses for the South or for slavery. Only the tariff was inimical to Southern

---

24. For accounts that emphasize these factors in Republican propaganda, see Glyndon G. VanDeusen, "Why the Republican Party Came to Power," in *The Crisis of the Union*, ed. George Harmon Knoles (Baton Rouge: Louisiana State University Press), pp. 3–20, and Barrington Moore, p. 130.

interests, but on this issue the South and her Northern allies had been doing well and could expect to continue to fend off protariff forces within the Union.

These observations suggest the severe limits of an economic explanation for the war that focuses on Northern interests. However, there is one point that is important to retain: namely, that for reasons largely independent of the slavery issue, a political coalition was emerging in which the South had no essential place. There was no political reason for the Republican leaders to soften their rhetoric to accommodate Southern feelings, nothing to dissuade them from broadening their appeal to include both the negrophobic self-interest of western farmers and miners, and the moralistic fervor of the abolitionists. Many scholars now hold that the appeal of the Republican party was not only largely independent of concern over slavery, but substantially independent of national issues generally, being much more a function of local, cultural, and religious concerns.[25] These arguments have not been without their critics,[26] but it is noteworthy that no such claims have emerged with respect to the South, where concern for national politics was intense and widespread.

Thus, the table turns back to the South, and the question becomes why that region reacted "in direct and exaggerated response to the apparent growth of abolitionism among the Northern people." [27] Why did the South engage in "a series of constantly mounting demands for symbolic acts by which the North would say that slavery was all right?" [28] Surely this behavior constitutes a *prima facie* case for an explanation

25. Perhaps the best of the studies supporting this view is Ronald P. Formisano, *The Birth of Mass Political Parties: Michigan, 1827–1861* (Princeton: Princeton University Press, 1971).

26. Eric Foner, "Causes of the Civil War;" Richard B. Latner and Peter Levine, "Perspectives on Antebellum Pietistic Politics," *Reviews in American History* 4 (March 1976).

27. Steven Channing, *Crisis of Fear*, p. 71. See also pp. 130, 187, 213–14.

28. Charles G. Sellers, Jr., "Comments on Why the Southern States Seceded," in Knoles, p. 88.

based on paranoia and guilt,[29] emotional racism and "the basic fear of the Negro," [30] or the conspiratorial machinations of "a small group of elite Southerners" consciously trying to escalate regional conflict.[31] We shall show that these symbolic actions did, in certain respects, make economic sense for slaveowners. But first we have to inquire again into the nature of their economic attachment to slavery.

The Profitability of Slavery Once More

If the profitability of slavery is accepted, explanations based specifically on the notion that slaveowners were losing money can be ruled out. But this agreement does not take us far, and the precise meaning of the statement "slavery was profitable" makes a great deal of difference. Following Conrad and Meyer, a number of studies have attempted to estimate the rate of return on investment in slave property by comparing the market price of slaves to a hypothetical stream of returns over a hypothetical future.[32] As Yasuba and Sutch argued, this is no test of the viability of slavery, but only a measure of the appropriateness of the capitalization of the income stream—a test that can never be conclusive, once we recall that the income stream is a hypothetical expected one. Yasuba's analysis is depicted in Figure 5.1: in each year the price of slaves is determined by the interaction of a demand curve with an inelastic supply curve, because, after the closing of the African slave trade, the aggregate slave labor supply could not be increased in response to higher prices, except over time. The observed slave price was in fact well

29. David B. Davis, *The Slave Power Conspiracy and the Paranoid Style*; Charles G. Sellers, Jr., "The Travail of Slavery."
30. Channing, p. 264. The classic statement is Ulrich B. Phillips, "The Central Theme of Southern History," *American Historical Review* 24 (October 1928).
31. Benson, pp. 316–22. Benson stresses as well the development of "authoritarian" character traits among slaveholders and the "radically defective" federal constitution.
32. See Hugh Aitken, ed., *Did Slavery Pay?*

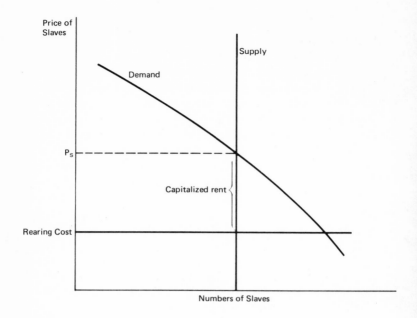

FIGURE 5.1. *Determination of Price of Slaves*

above the long-run cost of rearing new slaves, and the difference between the two accrued as a capitalized rent to the owner of the slave at the time of birth. Slave prices rose steadily over time, to levels far above the rearing cost, and indeed were never higher than on the eve of the Civil War.[33]

The point is not just that the real proof of profitability is the high slave prices themselves, but that the rising profitability is *embodied* in the higher prices. In the abstract, there is little point in sharply differentiating between the slaveholders' interest in annual earnings on his crops and in the value of his slave property, because slave prices will reflect the expected stream of future earnings from the use of slave labor. For similar reasons, economists frequently use

33. For simplicity, the diagram abstracts from the dimension of *time,* but of course each year's rearing costs must be appropriately compounded to reflect the interval between birth and prime age (if this is the standard).

the change in land values as a measure of the benefits of transportation improvements.[34] In reality, of course, there was great variability among slaveholders in realized earnings and presumably in expectations as well; but the capital gains from rising slave prices were sufficient to make financial successes of all but the most incompetent slaveowners. The fact is that virtually every slaveholder who was careful enough to keep his slaves alive made at least a normal profit during the 1850s from capital gains alone.[35] One may argue that these slave prices were too high, and that they would have had to fall (as implied by the evidence of the previous chapter), but there is no gainsaying the historical fact that up to the moment of secession, slaveholders' wealth had continued to grow to levels that were truly staggering in comparison with the average wealth of any other significant group in the population. Some historians continue to advance the absurd proposition that slaveholders were being "squeezed" by high slave prices, and that the development created a divergence of interest between "young, rising slaveholders" and "older, established" slaveholders.[36] Slaves were bought and slaves were sold, but slaveholders as a class were being enriched, and even the smallest holder would find his financial portfolio dominated by the value of his slave property. Of course, the higher prices meant that non-slaveholders had more difficult access to the slaveowning class: but this was at most an opportunity foregone or deferred, and however resentful they might have felt about their position, these were not the men who made the secessionist revolution.

Once we understand that the essence of the profitability

34. For example, Robert W. Fogel, *The Union Pacific Railroad* (Baltimore: Johns Hopkins Press, 1960).

35. The importance of capital gains in the profitability of slavery is stressed by Richard Sutch, "The Profitability of Ante Bellum Slavery—Revisited," *Southern Economic Journal* 31 (April 1965), and by Richard K. Vedder, David C. Klingaman, and Lowell E. Galloway, "The Profitability of Ante-Bellum Agriculture in the Cotton Belt: Some New Evidence," *Atlantic Economic Journal* 2 (November 1974).

36. Barney, p. 93ff.

of slavery was the financial value of slave property, certain things fall into place. One implication is that profitability was enjoyed by every slaveholder, large and small, in every part of the South. The reasons for the high prices have to do with trends in cotton, but the capital gains extended to owners who had nothing to do with cotton—because, unlike land and unlike free labor, slaves were moveable and saleable and their value was determined in an efficient region-wide market independently of local crops, local productivity, and local development. To some historians it may seem self-evident that profitability studies that emphasize regional distinctions and variations are more sophisticated than an aggregate analysis,[37] but in this case the most fundamental elements of the profitability are aggregate in their very nature. The value of slave property was a great unifying factor for the South, and an economic interest, largely separate from the interest in the success of southern agriculture, developed around these values. Edward Phifer, a close student of slaveowners' thinking, makes the following observation:

> One thing which has tended to lead scholars astray in their analysis of the economics of slavery has been their failure to probe the mind of the slaveholder. What must be understood is that the slaveholder was not at heart an investor; he was a speculator. His primary interest was not in yearly income on an investment; his primary interest was in appreciation . . . [T]hrough capital accumulation he hoped to endow his progeny for generations to come.[38]

37. See, for example, Richard Wade's comparisons of Fogel and Engerman with Lewis C. Gray: "He said it in a much more sophisticated fashion; it was profitable where you had good land and good management. Slavery was less profitable in South Carolina than it was up the Red River. To me that was a much more sophisticated way of doing it." Bruce Stave, "A Conversation with Richard C. Wade," *Journal of Urban History* 3 (February 1977).

38. Edward Phifer, "Slavery in Microcosm."

In context, it is clear that Phifer does not mean to suggest that slaveholders were looking for a quick sale, nor that they had no concern for yearly output: the situation envisaged is perhaps similar to homeownership today—most families buy one house to live in and do not frequently buy and sell in response to fluctuations in price; yet these households maintain an active and sometimes intense interest in the value of their homes.

Phifer was writing about Burke County, North Carolina: does his statement merely reflect the outlook of those in the slave-breeding states of the Old South? Certainly the relative importance of capital gains was not the same everywhere, but there is evidence that the differences between Southeast and Southwest were not great in this respect,[39] and it is a fundamental error to believe that southwestern slaveowners had a countervailing interest in low slave prices. As we shall see, their political behavior reveals an equally intense concern for maintaining slave values. Across the South, slaveholders formed a class of great wealth with a distinctive unity of economic interest—not necessarily on policies concerning the economics of slavery, but in slavery itself. One notes the contrast with the farmers' movement of the late nineteenth century, for which unity was impossible because farmers' financial situations and economic interests varied widely, depending on crops, location, distance to markets, etc. The slave South had a unifying economic interest that transcended differences such as these. It is difficult to think of historical cases that are remotely comparable,[40] and so perhaps it should not be altogether surprising that the result-

39. Fogel and Engerman's formulation of the question is not precisely the same, but their evidence is relevant (*Time on the Cross*, pp. 79–82). Our discussion has no implications for the debate over "slave-breeding," or planters efforts to increase fertility.

40. Olsen writes that "race slavery in the American South may have created one of the largest percentage groups of investors in the direct exploitation of labor that the world has ever seen," but he does not go on to stress the unified character of the determination of the value of that property. See Otto Olsen, "Historians and the Extent of Slave Ownership in the Southern United States," p. 113.

ing political behavior reflects a different logic from that which we are used to.

The evidence does support the view that secession was essentially a slaveholders' movement. Ralph A. Wooster has exhaustively tracked down 1,780 of the 1,859 delegates to the fifteen secession conventions of 1860–61. He found that delegates voting for secession were more likely to be slaveholders than those voting against, but this difference was not nearly as decisive as the striking correlation between the proportion of slaves in a county's population and the likelihood of that county's voting for secession.[41] However, there is little basis in Wooster's evidence for a claim that large slaveholders were more likely to favor secession than small. Almost all of the opposition to secession came from counties with very few slaves. Granted that each state had a political setting of its own and that, in some of these, certain nonslaveholding areas may have cast the key votes; nonetheless, when the issue came down to a vote, it was clear enough where the slaveholders stood.

Making Economic Sense of the Politics of Slavery

The task of explaining the apparently irrational policies of secession and the regional aggressiveness that led up to secession remains. To understand the logic of this behavior, we have to remember that the price of slaves did not reflect an observable intrinsic value of slave labor, but an expectation of future returns. With slave values so far above cost-determined levels, it is no exaggeration to say that the determination of slave prices was essentially a psychological matter, albeit a psychology influenced by trends in cotton prices and production. The value of slave property was highly sensitive to changes in expectations, not so much in

41. Ralph A. Wooster, *The Secession Conventions of the South*. See also Michael P. Johnson, *Towards a Patriarchal Republic: The Secession of Georgia* (Baton Rouge: Louisiana State University Press, 1977), esp. Appendix.

erratic year-to-year movements as in slower changes in long-term expectations about the future. Fogel and Engerman's calculations contain the important implication that three-fourths of the slave price rise in the lower South between the late 1840s and the late 1850s is attributable to changes in expectations.[42] The two distinctive dimensions of slave values—their psychological nature and their region-wide character—are essential to understanding the political behavior of slaveowners. They imply that every political discussion of slavery was an event that could affect the value of every slaveholders' property. Slaveholders had to worry, not just about the objective reality of Northern threats to slavery, but about the fears of these attacks harbored by their fellow owners.

This is very different from an argument based on slave-holder pessimism about the economic and political future. In light of the high and rising slave prices, so heavily weighted by expectations and confidence, it is difficult to credit interpretations based on a "mood of despair," a "sense of desperation," or even an "uneasiness about economic prospects" at the time of secession.[43] If it is thought unreasonably abstract and simplified to subsume all Southern expectations into one "index of sanguinity," it should also be recorded that every systematic survey of opinion in the 1850s finds that expectations were favorable.[44] A wide range of opinions may be found, but "in sheer numbers the opti-

42. "The Economics of Slavery," p. 33. See also *Time on the Cross,* pp. 103–6.
43. Barney, pp. 19–20, 222; Genovese, *Political Economy,* p. 284.
44. William J. Cooper, "The Cotton Crisis in the Antebellum South," pp. 383–86, surveys the leading agricultural journals. A similar prognosis of "an era of expansion and unrivaled commercial prosperity" is found in Percy L. Rainwater, "Economic Benefits of Secession." Rainwater's argument is somewhat ambiguous on the issue of expansion: he asserts that most Mississippians thought that slavery required extension, but he does not distinguish a general posture of aggressiveness on this issue (as discussed below) from the specific question of the need for land. Cooper found that "writers in these journals had few doubts that ample productive cotton land remained within Southern borders." (p. 384).

mists dwarf the pessimists," and the majority entered secession contemplating the "Great and Increased Prosperity of
the South and the Brilliant Future Which Is Opening Upon
Her." [45] Genovese argues that slaveowners were not
moved as much by narrow economic interest as by their
commitment to maintaining a whole complex of social relationships; but it is difficult to distinguish broad from narrow
motives when the two agree, as they do in this case, and it
seems clear that most slaveowners did not feel pressured to
choose between class preservation and immediate economic
interests. As Professor McCay of South Carolina wrote on the
eve of the Civil War: "Never before has the planting been
more profitable than in the last few years . . . the planters
have been everywhere rich, prosperous and happy." [46]

The only dark cloud on the horizon was the threat of interference with slavery by the North. But slave prices reflected expectations with respect to the political as well as
the economic future of slavery. Undoubtedly some slaveowners believed that Lincoln or a more radical successor
meant to tamper with slavery; but to the extent that they
did so believe, the evidence suggests that they did not fear
Lincoln would be successful. They believed, in other words,
that secession would succeed, and many believed that it
would succeed peacefully. The main pillar under these be-
liefs was King Cotton thinking—the notion that the South,
"safely entrenched behind her cotton bags . . . can defy the
world—for the civilized world depends on the cotton of the
South." [47] Secessionist convention debate revealed widespread

45. This and similar titles appeared in *DeBow's Review* in the late
1850s. Cf. Cooper, pp. 384–85.
46. C. F. McCay, "Cultivation of Cotton." The editor notes that
the article was "written before the war" (p. 103).
47. *Vicksburg Sun*, November 12, 1860, quoted in Rainwater, *Mississippi, Storm Center of Secession 1856–1861*, p. 164. See also *American Farmer* 1 (April 1860), p. 316; *DeBow's Review* 26 (January 1859),
p. 229. Owsley found that the King Cotton theory was "universally accepted in the Southern states by 1860" and "unquestionably . . . was
decisive in precipitating secession." See "The Confederacy and King
Cotton," *North Carolina Historical Review* 6 (October 1929).

acceptance of the idea that the North could not possibly risk war on cotton, and, if she did, England would have to intervene on the side of the South. Some historians seem to believe that these arguments were largely concocted by secessionist agitators who did not really believe them,[48] but even if this were so, the assurances were effective. Channing asserts that the overwhelming majority of South Carolinians believed in the imminence of a peaceful acquiescence by the North. As Mrs. Caroline Gilman wrote to her daughters in 1860, "Civil War was *foreign to the original plan*." [49]

The explanation for secession, then, is simply that slaveholders owned extremely valuable property and were not only enjoying prosperity but expected their good fortune to continue; the only serious threat to this situation was Northern interference with slavery; and it was widely believed that a straightforward safeguard against such interference was available—peaceful secession. On the basis of this evidence, we cannot and do not wish to rule out the contention that events were influenced by the actions of an elite minority, which consciously desired separation for irrational reasons or which did harbor long-run fears about the viability of slavery in the Union. But if this is the case, we can still say that the social basis for the success of their movement was the optimistic outlook of the majority. These judgments were of course mistaken, but they were based on a rational reading of the objective situation, and were supported by the extreme fears often voiced in England about the implications of a cutoff of cotton supply,[50] and by the assurances of noninterference that flowed in from the "very highest political circles of the North." [51] They also rested on the accurate perception that the North had no strong economic reasons to

48. Barney, pp. 234–35. Rainwater, however, found that "a very few only of the secession leaders believed that war would result from disunion" (*Mississippi*, p. 191).

49. Channing, pp. 274, 280.

50. For example, see Arthur W. Silver, *Manchester Men and Indian Cotton 1847–1872* (Manchester: The University Press, 1966), chap. 2.

51. Channing, pp. 274–76.

fight a war over slavery. Explaining the postsecession response of the North is more of a challenge to an economic historian than explaining secession itself.

But it is misleading to focus only on the prosperous year of 1860, because the political crisis of that year was only the culmination of years of bitter intersectional conflict. We still have to explain why Southerners went to extremes in insisting on absolute guarantees of their rights by the federal government everywhere in the Union. Why did they help to create an antislavery monster by brazenly chasing a handful of runaway slaves around the country, when the fugitive issue was acknowledged to be "not of the slightest consequence" as a practical matter.[52] Why were they bent on squashing the slightest murmur of antislavery sentiment in the South? With so much to conserve, why weren't they more conservative?

Even these extremes of Southern behavior may be viewed as consistent with the basically economic motive of maintaining the value of slave property, when we remember that the value of slave property was so thoroughly dependent on expectations and confidence. Such a financial asset involves external effects of region-wide scope: even if *I* attach no importance whatsoever to fugitive slave legislation as it effects my own slaves, if I think that *you* (any nontrivial number of slaveowners or buyers) attach some importance to it, then the issue affects me financially and I have good reason to become a political advocate of strong guarantees. Thus, slaveowner concern for symbolic issues and remote territorial affairs need not reflect exaggerated fears of a general breakdown of slave discipline or hypersensitivity to inferred slights on their character, but immediate financial concern for the value of their property. Consider, for example, the following quotation from the *Charleston Mercury* (October 11, 1860), on the effects of the election of a Republican president:

52. By the radical *Charleston Mercury*, quoted in Sellers, "Comments," p. 89.

. . . thousands of slaveholders will despair of the institution. While the conditions of things in the [border] states will force their slaves on the markets of the cotton states, the timid of the cotton states will also sell their slaves. The general distrust, must affect purchasers. The consequence must be, slave property must be greatly depreciated. . . . We suppose, that taking in view all these things, it is not extravagant to estimate, that the submission of the South to the administration of the Federal Government under Messrs. Lincoln and Hamlin, must reduce the value of slaves in the South, one hundred dollars each.

Note that the writer makes no assertion about what Lincoln would do, and obviously believes that actual difficulties would be faced only on the border: but the $100 loss would be felt by every single slaveholder.

The closest analogy today is the behavior of homeowners. A house is typically the largest asset owned by a family—indeed families are usually heavily in debt if they buy a house —and here also the value of the property depends on the opinions and prejudices of others. In this case as well, prejudice and intolerance are intensified by market forces. *I* may not really care whether a black family moves next door, but, if I feel that others care, I will be under financial pressure to share their views or at least to act as though I do.[53] The main differences between the housing case and slavery are that many owners held more than one slave, and that for slavery these were not "neighborhood effects" limited to a small geographic area but system-wide externalities, so that a threat to slavery anywhere was a threat to slaveowners everywhere. The effect was to greatly exacerbate the response to any threat.

53. See Luigi Laurenti, *Property Values and Race* (Berkeley: University of California Press, 1961), chaps. 1 and 2, for evidence of the widespread acceptance in housing-market circles of the belief that blacks lower property values. Note that these views are maintained, despite the absence of evidence of actual negative effects on property values (chap. 3).

Once this mechanism is understood, it begins to make economic sense for the South to have been so concerned with the letter of the law, and it becomes more understandable that slavery could not stand criticism on moral grounds. The strength of the argument is that it is not based on an exclusively economic nor exclusively rational conception of motivation and behavior. Fears, racism, misperceptions, and long-run strategic calculations all undoubtedly did exist.[54] The point is that economic forces served to intensify every other motive for the South's insistence on guarantees of the rights of slaveholders and even the quest for a virtual moral endorsement of slavery by the North. The argument does not imply that Southern politicians were scrutinizing slave prices in their every action; but the widespread concern over property values created a situation in which an ambitious politician could easily mobilize a constituency by strongly insisting on absolute guarantees for slaveowners' rights. And was it coincidental that the suppression of internal antislavery opinion coincided, not just with the rise of abolitionism, but with the first great boom in cotton and slave prices in the mid-1830s?

Reopening the Slave Trade as a Test Case

One issue that tested slaveowners' loyalty to their broader class interests as opposed to their property values was reopening the external slave trade. The fate of the campaign for reopening offers an interesting contrast to the campaign for secession, to which it bears similarities. Both were part of the radical Southern Rights movement of the 1850s, and many viewed reopening the trade as simply a logical corollary to the moral defense of slavery. As Representative Miles

54. The argument has obvious applicability to fears of slave rebellion in the South, but it may be less important than the fact that even unsuccessful rebellion could be fatal to members of a particular family. In part then, this behavior is akin to the "paranoia" about urban crime today, a phenomenon that could hardly be considered pathological in any clinical sense.

put it in 1859, the anti-slave trade laws "stamp the people of my section as pirates, and put a stigma upon their institutions." [55] So here was another symbolic issue of principle, and in this case it is quite clear that a small group of radicals agitated the issue in the conscious hope that the idea would be so unpalatable to the North that secession would be hastened.[56] Furthermore, a strong case was made that reopening the trade would strengthen the political foundations of slavery in several ways: it would increase representation in Congress, increase the slaveholding fraction of the white population, arrest the relative decline of slavery in the upper South, and hasten the westward expansion of slavery into areas not yet dominated by Northerners.[57]

Despite all these elements to recommend the issue, it did not escape the attention of slaveholders that the proposal to reopen was a proposal to lower the price of slaves. No test case is perfect, and one can certainly think of other reasons to oppose reopening. But the threat to slave prices was of intense concern to slaveholders all over the South, and the failure of the campaign is entirely consistent with our analysis. No coastal state ever repealed its own laws against the importation of slaves, and no legislature passed a resolution even on the symbolic issue of repealing federal prohibitions. Politicians like Barnwell and Rhett, who initially seized on the issue to advance their careers, subsequently moved away from it. It is not surprising that the border states opposed reopening, but the proposal was defeated almost as decisively in every one of the states of the lower South and Southwest. In Georgia, according to Alexander Stephens, the people were "as much opposed to it as they are at the North." [58] In Alabama, the issue was seldom men-

55. Quoted in Ronald Takaki, p. 72. See also chap. 2 and pp. 68–72.

56. *Ibid.*, p. 27. Barton J. Bernstein, "Southern Politics and Attempts to Reopen the African Slave Trade," pp. 25–26; Russel, p. 216.

57. Rainwater, *Mississippi*, pp. 70–76; Russel, *Economic Aspects*, pp. 217–18; Takaki, pp. 33–67; Bernstein, pp. 19–20; *DeBow's Review* 26 (June 1859), p. 654; 27 (August 1859), p. 208.

58. Quoted in Harvey Wish, "The Revival of the African Slave Trade in the United States, 1856–1860," p. 581.

tioned outside of the Southern Commercial Conventions.[59] In Mississippi and Louisiana, periods of intense agitation around the issue were followed by an ebbing and subsiding, well before secession and well before the exigencies of foreign relations dictated caution.[60] Even in Texas, the Democratic party convention squashed a slave trade resolution by a vote of 221 to 81; despite this clear-cut party position, Texas voters went on to elect Sam Houston over the "regular" Democratic candidate for governor, because it was "supposed" that this candidate supported reopening.[61] It was not a Virginian, but H. S. Foote of Mississippi, who countered the class-preservation argument for reopening with the following telling statement.[62]

> If the price of slaves comes down, then the permanency of the institution comes down. Why? Because every man values his property in proportion to its actual intrinsic worth. . . . Would you be willing to shoulder your musket in vindication of slaveholding rights . . . if your slaves were only worth five dollars apiece? Why, every man sees that that is an absurdity. Therefore, the permanence of the system depends on keeping the prices high.

The geographical concentration of slavery was ultimately of some importance in determining the outcome of the war, but before the war the risks of political isolation were less

---

59. Clarence Phillips Denman, *The Secession Movement in Alabama*, p. 72.

60. Wish, p. 580; James Paisley Hendrix, Jr., "The Efforts to Reopen the African Slave Trade in Louisiana." Hendrix shows that the issue in Louisiana was a transitory one involving personalities and promotion by a prospective slave-importing firm; the lines of division on the slave trade were not closely associated with basic economic divisions or with the vote on secession. Note, however, that Hendrix mistakenly downplays the fear of a fall in slave prices on the grounds that cotton and sugar interests were prosperous in the 1850s.

61. Bernstein, "Southern Politics," p. 34.

62. *DeBow's Review* 27 (August 1859), p. 219.

worrisome to slaveholders than immediate threats to the value of their property.[63]

It is not altogether surprising that many historians have missed this pervasive logic, since it seems to have been widely believed in the North *and* in the border states that reopening was a chief object of secession. This perception was utterly incorrect: not only had secessionist convention candidates given early assurance that it was not intended, but some Deep Southerners were so shortsighted in pursuit of capital gains that they saw no particular need to include any additional slave states in the new confederation.[64] The belief that the confederacy would reopen the trade was one reason for the initial border state reluctance to join the movement. What they found, however, was that the Montgomery Constitution of 1861 *outlawed* the African trade and went so far as to authorize the Congress to prohibit the importation of slaves from the United States! While these measures had obvious tactical purposes with respect to the border states and Europe, the prior political history leaves little doubt that they reflected the political preferences of slaveholders in all states: for example, after voting for secession by 84 to 15, the Mississippi convention voted down a resolution for reopening by 66 to 13.[65] As a coercive measure directed at the border states it was remarkably successful. As J. Randolph Tucker of Virginia argued: "If we do

63. There is evidence that the early slave-trade closings were at times attributable to efforts to shore up slave values. See Gray, p. 357; David B. Davis, *The Problem of Slavery in Western Culture*, p. 141. Gray (pp. 616–17) explains the Southern acceptance of the agreement closing the slave trade in the 1790s in terms of low slave prices, an argument that receives some support in Robert McColley, *Slavery and Jeffersonian Virginia* (Urbana: University of Illinois Press, 1964), pp. 117, 163, 170. William W. Freehling, "The Founding Fathers and Slavery," points to geographic concentration—attributable in part to the slave-trade closing—as an important factor in slavery's ultimate undoing. It may be stretching the point, however, to give the Founding Fathers any credit for this factor, since the slaveowners themselves discussed the matter many times and never took any steps to reopen the trade.

64. Russel, *Economic Aspects*, pp. 268–70.

65. Wooster, *Secession Conventions*, pp. 37, 48.

not go with the cotton states, our $250,000,000 of slave property would perish." [66]

Conclusion:
Northern Expansion and Southern Psychology

The establishment of slave prices above reproduction costs is a decisive historical feature of slavery in the United States. This situation is frequently listed as an explanation of some distinctive economic aspects of U.S. slavery—the high growth rates of the slave population, the comparatively favorable material treatment of slaves, and the relative infrequency of voluntary manumission. This chapter argues that the nature of American slave prices had pervasive effects on political life as well, creating an economic stake in slaves as valuable property, as opposed to the more general stake in cotton agriculture under slavery, and converting every minor threat to the institution into a direct financial threat to slaveholders everywhere in the United States. The fact that slaveowning classes in other countries employed slaves with prices much closer to reproduction or importation costs may explain why they displayed more of a "take-the-money-and-run" philosophy when slave systems came under attack.[67] In the North, the motives of property accumulation and property-value augmentation generated an ethos of expansion, promotion, land speculation, and labor recruitment. In the South, the same motives in a different institutional setting fostered an insatiable thirst for psychological reassurance.

The relationship between these two political lines is illustrated by their intersection at the time of the Kansas-

---

66. Quoted in Russel, *Economic Aspects*, p. 281.
67. Genovese points to the contrast with the slaveowner-capitalists of Cuba, who manifested no fundamental class identity with slaveowners in the United States when they sided with the North during the war in the hope that the Louisiana sugar industry would be destroyed. See *The World the Slaveholders Made*, pp. 70–71.

Nebraska crisis in 1854.[68] The plan of Stephen A. Douglas to organize the area west of Missouri and Iowa as the Nebraska Territory was only one of many plans whose clear initial purpose was to facilitate the building of a railroad westward through the region. Contrary to later allegations that he developed the scheme in a corrupt bargain for the presidency, Douglas had extensive personal real estate investments which would benefit from the railroad, and his backing and support came from Illinois interests with similar positions. But because of the multiplicity of plans, no one route could command a majority, and Douglas found that he needed the support of Southern senators. Their price was essentially symbolic: the repeal of the Missouri Compromise prohibiting slavery north of 36°31'. Since Douglas was sure slavery would in fact be excluded from both Kansas and Nebraska by the voters in those territories,[69] he thought he was trading symbol for substance, and it must have seemed an ideal bargain. It was an arrangement that grew naturally out of the underlying property systems of both regions.

Instead of bringing peace, however, the Kansas-Nebraska bill brought a colossal uproar in the North. The crux of the problem was that at the time of uncertain status for slavery in the territories, the South's craving for reassurance of the legitimacy of slavery seemed to constitute a threat to the basic material interests and ambitions of Northerners. Correspondingly, each new decision for free territorial status was seen by the South as a moral rebuke to slavery, hence a threat to the foundations of Southern wealth. Although it would seem that an objective basis for regional compromise existed, guaranteed security for slave property in exchange for the unfettered free development of the territories, it was

68. This paragraph is based on chap. 7 in David M. Potter, *The Impending Crisis 1848–1861.*

69. The creation of two territories, Kansas in the South and Nebraska in the North, was apparently without ulterior motives, but was widely interpreted at the time as an effort to divide the territory into free and slave areas. Potter, p. 160.

in the nature of things that such a settlement was extremely difficult to achieve.

No investigation is attempted here of the Northern decision to refuse to accept peaceful Southern secession, except to say that, unlike the opposition to the extension of slavery, it does not seem to have emanated from the force of mass political sentiments and pressures, as secession did in the South. The Northern response could not have been based on an intense desire to eradicate slavery: a bare one-third of the Congress blocked Lincoln's effort to put through a constitutional amendment guaranteeing the perpetuation of slavery in the existing slave states. Certainly economic concerns entered into the thinking of Lincoln and his advisors, as well as political, nationalistic, and perhaps even moral and idealistic motives. But these decisions must be studied at the level of small-group behavior, albeit behavior influenced by perceptions of a social background; it was only after the first shots were fired that a genuinely popular opinion crystallized in support of military measures to preserve the Union.

The moral sensitivities of both regions would have made it difficult at any time to achieve a stable arrangement satisfactory to each. But many of these barriers to agreement were at their historical maxima in the 1850s: slave prices were at all-time highs, magnifying the Southern financial stake in the moral issues; a broad geographic area was being rapidly settled and brought into territorial status, raising unavoidable political issues on which it was difficult to satisfy both sides; and the North continued to be dominated politically by family farmers and landowners, not yet by the industrial capitalist interests that matured at the end of the century. One might stress the disproportionate influence that the character of slave property values bestowed upon abolitionist agitation, but reform groups did not exhibit much staying power or political effectiveness on behalf of the freedmen when they were no longer allied with important economic interest groups. As slave prices fell and cotton receded in prominence, Southern vulnerability to rhetorical attacks might have diminished as well. If this analysis is correct, then the missed opportunities for delay and compromise during 1859–61 loom larger and larger historically. But as difficult as the proposition is for twentieth-century Americans to accept, it was slavery as well as the Union that would have been preserved for a long time. Slavery would have faced internal political and economic pressures in the South, but the notion that slavery would have faded away peacefully in the late nineteenth century has always been a wishful chapter in historical fiction, not part of a plausible counterfactual history.[70]

70. Compare the career of slavery in MacKinlay Kantor's *If the South Had Won the Civil War* (New York: Bantam, 1961) with that of Edmund Ruffin in *Anticipations of the Future* (Richmond: J. W. Randolph, 1860).

6

After the War

By the time of the Compromise of 1876, no Southern leader could believe that the South held "the lever which moves or stops the great car of commerce." [1] The South had suffered defeat and devastation, and had been through a decade of disruption and turmoil in politics and agricultural organization; but cotton's loss of status and leverage in world affairs would have occurred even if none of these dramatic events had taken place, and the South's own position would have followed cotton in decline. Impressed by the loss of the South's market share, some Southerners of the late 1860s and early 1870s blamed the rise of foreign competition, a theme that has attracted some modern followers.[2] But foreign competition was not the problem: cotton prices were high by historical standards during 1866–79, as American cotton continued to exert a dominant influence on the world price (Figure 4.2). When American cotton recovered, the price re-

1. *DeBow's Review* 26 (February 1859), p. 229.
2. *DeBow's Review*, After the War Series (AWS), vol. 4 (November 1867) p. 450 ". . . the unwelcome truth is forced upon us that our prestige as a great and controlling cotton power, is passing away from us forever." See also *DeBow's Review* 5 (January 1868), pp. 82–86; (February 1868), pp. 186–88; (March 1868), pp. 225–49; Alfred H. Conrad and John R. Meyer, "Slavery as an Obstacle to Economic Growth in the United States," *Journal of Economic History* 27 (December 1967), pp. 528–29; Hugh Aitken, ed., *Did Slavery Pay?* pp. 273–74, 284–85, 288.

turned to normal, but with the rate of expansion slowed to a fraction of its prewar level.[3] The mistaken crediting of ante-bellum progress to dynamic characteristics of the South is sometimes repeated in relationship to the two decades after 1900: Southern per capita income did rise faster than the national average during 1900–1920 (for that matter during 1880–1920, since there was only slight relative retrogression between 1880 and 1900), but these gains were just as vulner-able as those of 1860. When cotton markets languished in the 1920s, most of the relative gain was lost. The Southern economy was by no means utterly stagnant during this period, but the progress of industry was not rapid enough to outweigh the swings in cotton demand, and more than a half-century after Reconstruction the region had made vir-tually no progress toward the national mean. It means little to say that the South grew "as fast as the rest of the country," if the calculation starts from the nadir of Southern economic history. Even during the later period of cotton prosperity the industrial focus of world capitalism had moved well beyond textiles, and the South's position in national and world eco-nomic life was a pale shadow of its former self.

Taking a long view of Southern history, we can describe the origins of the regional economic problem rather simply: the extended cotton boom of the first Industrial Revolution brought a rapid settlement and expansion of a region uniquely suited to cotton production. When the boom was over, this population found itself on land that could produce little else commercially, and, in fact, the earliest-settled areas turned out to be distinctly inferior even for cotton. In com-bination with continued demographic growth and limited

3. I have shown elsewhere that most of the expanded cotton pro-duction in Egypt, India, and Brazil can be explained by extrapolation of prewar supply curves in response to the extremely high prices of the 1860s; the expansion was in fact quickly reversed when prices fell. Continuation of the prewar demand expansion would have quickly swamped any effects of increased competition. See "Cotton Competition and the Postbellum Recovery of the American South," pp. 613–20, 630–32. Conversely, if there had been no change in cotton productivity, per capita cotton revenues would still have declined by more than 25 percent from 1860 to 1880.

out-migration, the end of the boom transformed the South within a generation from a society fundamentally organized around labor scarcity into a classic prototype of a labor-surplus region. This history might have been similar under any number of institutional and political systems, but, such as they were, the main opportunities for getting off this historical track were missed during the period before 1860, when cotton prosperity did not generate strong nonagricultural skills and activity. Given this legacy, it is doubtful that the choices open to the postbellum South could have made much difference for the region as a whole. Only the combination of massive out-migration and the application of modern technologies has produced fundamental change in this economic picture in the twentieth century.

But if we take a less distant view, the details of postbellum history remain interesting. The South and the nation did have political choices concerning legal protection and the distribution of land to the freedmen, and Southern farmers made microeconomic choices in crops and organization. The effects of these decisions on the regional economy were not negligible, and their effects on human welfare in broadest terms were substantial indeed. This chapter explores some of the most prominent changes, looking backward to the antebellum patterns for contrast and perspective.

The Rise of Tenancy

Numerous accounts and descriptions of the transition to a free labor system after the war exist, but we will probably never have a good quantitative knowledge of these developments. There are no reliable figures on farm tenancy before the census of 1880, and, even at that time, some of the most basic questions about tenure systems were not asked. Furthermore, much of the literary material on postwar changes is colored by an unsympathetic, unperceptive, and judgmental posture toward the behavior of the freed slaves. For example, the departure of former slaves from the plantation for the towns and other parts of the South was frequently attributed by observers to an ignorant euphoria over emancipation and to fantasies of "forty acres and a mule." More sympathetic writers have noted that expectations of a land-distribution program had been actively encouraged by federal authorities, and that much of the mobility represented efforts to reunite families that had been separated under slavery.[4]

Nonetheless, some essential facts do seem established. One of the most important is that despite the reports of distress plantation sales and despite the decline in average farm size reported in the 1870 census, there was no basic change in the concentration of land ownership.[5] Antebellum holdings were not really broken up in favor of either blacks or white nonslaveholders, and most of the new small farms were tenancies of one kind or another. Secondly, the characteristic forms of black tenancy emerged only after several years of institutional experimentation, beginning with efforts to re-establish the essentials of antebellum plantation organization on a wage-paying basis. The fact that these attempts were failures is historically instructive, confirming the essential connection between slavery and large-scale agriculture. Unfortunately, as with most "natural" historical experiments of this sort, wage-paying plantations were unsatisfactory for more reasons than one. On the one hand, as the planters saw it, was the tendency of the freedmen to "use too freely their newly-found liberty" [6]—i.e., the emergence of the standard problems of retaining and managing non-family labor, universally characteristic of American agriculture. On

4. On the responsibility of federal authorities for expectations of land distribution, see William S. McFeely, *Yankee Stepfather: General O. O. Howard and the Freedmen* (New York: W. W. Norton & Co., Norton Library, 1970), esp. chap. 5.
    5. Roger W. Shugg, *Origins of Class Struggle in Louisiana*, chap. 8; Roger Ransom and Richard Sutch, *One Kind of Freedom*, chap. 4; Jonathan M. Wiener, "Planter-Merchant Conflict in Reconstruction Alabama," pp. 73–80.
    6. *Annual Report of the Commissioner of Agriculture 1867* (Washington, D.C.: Government Printing Office, 1867), p. 416.

the other side was the fact that "most of the Negroes next to owning the land themselves, preferred to rent," [7] hoping to achieve some degree of independence for their household and to organize their labor around the family, as was also typical of most American farming. Even those who described blacks as "unambitious of accumulation," noted that "the freedman . . . shows great anxiety to have his little home, with his horse, cow and hogs separate and apart from others." [8]

Observing the efforts by planters to restrict the freedom and mobility of black laborers through legal and extralegal means,[9] and observing also the oppressions and indignities that blacks suffered after the war, many historians have been tempted to say that very little *de facto* change had actually occurred since slavery. But it is important to recognize that the new systems of tenancy, as oppressive as they often came to be, represented a partial but genuine accommodation to the fact that black families were not willing to supply the same labor on the same terms that they had under slavery. A new locational pattern of housing emerged, much more decentralized onto separate plots of land.[10] Intrafamily division of labor moved toward the standard American pattern, as women left field work "to attend to the household and the garden." [11] What is not known is the full extent of decentralization in the actual operation of the plantation agriculture. It is generally conceded that sharecropping involved a substantially greater degree of planter influence and management than did straight tenancy, either for cash

7. Vernon Wharton, *The Negro in Mississippi 1865–1890*, pp. 63–64.

8. *DeBow's Review* (AWS), vol. 6 (July 1869), p. 609.

9. Efforts of this sort are surveyed in Stephen DeCanio, *Agriculture in the Postbellum South*, pp. 16–51. Activity of this kind is nearly universal in postemancipation societies. See W. Kloosterboer, *Involuntary Labour since the Abolition of Slavery* (Leiden: E. J. Brill, 1960).

10. See particularly the diagrams in Merle Prunty, "The Renaissance of the Southern Plantation," pp. 464, 467, 471, 473–74, 481–82.

11. *DeBow's Review* (AWS), vol. 6 (July 1869), p. 609. On this point, see Roger Ransom and Richard Sutch, "The Impact of the Civil War and of Emancipation on Southern Agriculture," pp. 13–14, 22–24.

or a fixed payment in crops. But some systems gave the sharecropper virtually complete automony once the contract was agreed; while on other plantations the plowing and planting was conducted "through and through" (i.e., jointly by the entire plantation labor force), leaving only cultivation and harvest to individual responsibility.[12] But even this system was a significant departure from slavery.

A third and most immediately pressing reason for dissatisfaction with the wage system was that the late 1860s were disastrous, productively and financially. Per capita cotton output was far below expectations, in part because of natural calamities, in larger part because the planters had not anticipated the extent of the labor problems they would experience after emancipation. At the same time, as production did expand along a stagnant and steeply-sloped demand curve, cotton prices fell precipitously—not to historically low levels, but to end-of-season levels which looked dismal in relation to wages and other outlays paid during the year.[13] The movement to a system "on shares" was attractive to the planters at this time as a means of sharing risks with their laborers, and as a means of economizing on cash outlays during a time of financial embarrassment and chaotic dislocation in Southern financial institutions. Some kind of share-arrangement may in many cases have been the only possible alternative for continued operation.

The history that is least well-known is that of the white farmers on small to medium-sized farms. Some writers have expressed the belief that the fall of land prices and the

12. Prunty, pp. 463–70. The gradual trend toward decentralized operations in the late 1860s is described in Peter Kolchin, *First Freedom*, pp. 35–48.

13. The dramatic fall in the cotton price brought an equally dramatic fall in wages by as much as 30 percent in one year alone (1867–68) (*Report of the Commissioner of Agriculture 1867*, p. 416). For graphic complaints about the effects of the price fall, see LaWanda Cox and John H. Cox, eds., *Reconstruction, The Negro and the New South* (New York: Harper & Row, 1973), pp. 331–33; *DeBow's Review* 3 (April-May 1867), p. 454; 5 (August 1869), pp. 785–87. A more thorough discussion of the rise of tenancy appears in Ransom and Sutch, *One Kind of Freedom*, chaps. 4 and 5.

withdrawal of black labor opened up new opportunities for small white farmers.[14] Nonetheless, by 1880 one-third of white farm operators in the cotton states were tenants;[15] it seems clear that this is a marked increase over the antebellum tenancy rate, but we know very little about when and how the increase occurred. There is little reason or evidence for believing that productivity actually fell on these farms. But one of the genuinely devastating effects of the Civil War was the destruction of more than one-third of the stock of hogs; even after fifteen years of recovery, the per capita level was little more than half of the antebellum figure.[16] Much of the burden of these losses fell on small white farmers,[17] and in combination with the trends in cotton during 1866–79, these circumstances led many of these people into a position with substantial similarities to that of the former slaves.

The Abandonment of Self-Sufficiency

By 1880, the South was no longer self-sufficient in basic foodstuffs. A trend toward greater specialization and less self-sufficiency is not surprising in agricultural history; but it is something of a challenge to explain why this particular

14. Enoch Marvin Banks, *The Economics of Land Tenure in Georgia*, esp. chap. 2; Matthew B. Hammond, *The Cotton Industry*, p. 129; Theodore Rosengarten, *All God's Dangers*, p. xvii.

15. Ransom and Sutch, "The Ex-Slave in the Post-Bellum South," pp. 132–33. This fact does not imply that white owners had actually lost title to their farms, only that farm proprietorships did not grow as fast as the farm-operator population. In the cotton states, the number of white owner-operated farms in 1880 is about 10 percent higher than the total number of farms in 1860.

16. Ransom and Sutch note that the 1870 census figure, which is two-thirds of the 1860 stock, may be too low because suckling pigs were omitted. But presumably the 1870 stock was in any case above that for 1865. See "Debt Peonage in the Cotton South After the Civil War," p. 657.

17. Forrest McDonald and Grady McWhiney, "The Antebellum Southern Herdsman, pp. 163–64.

development should have occurred during this particular two-decade period of virtual stagnation in cotton demand. The relative prices of cotton and foodstuffs were not very different in the late 1870s from those of the 1850s.[18] There were no dramatic changes in technology or yields; the emergence of the commercial fertilizer industry helped to extend the cotton frontier in the southeast, but in most parts of the South the abandonment of self-sufficiency predates the extensive use of commercial fertilizer.[19]

The precise extent of the shift in resource allocation is difficult to judge, because there are no data on acreage in specific crops before 1866. After the war, per capita production of all crops fell, and the continuance of self-sufficiency would have required some increase in the fraction of acreage devoted to food crops. Instead, the indications are that the shift was in the opposite direction. As we saw in chapter 4, the two census crops of 1850 and 1860 had roughly equal and opposite bias for cotton; the corn crop, however, seems to have been reasonably normal in both years.[20] The only other antebellum corn crop figures are the state-level esti-

18. The price of cotton divided by the price of corn averaged .153 in New Orleans during 1849 to 1860, and .148 in Charleston. For 1876–80, the on-farm relative price was .145 in Louisiana, .144 in South Carolina; computed from A. H. Cole, *Wholesale Commodity Prices in the United States 1700–1861*, Statistical Supplement (Cambridge: Harvard University Press, 1938), and U.S. Department of Agriculture, *Statistical Bulletin No. 16* (Washington, D.C.: Government Printing Office, June 1927).

19. Eugene A. Smith, in his report on Alabama for the 1880 census, wrote: "It may be said, in general terms, that in the great cotton-producing areas in Alabama the use of commercial fertilizers is comparatively unknown. In the regions of moderate production . . . the use of commercial fertilizers is gradually extending from east to west, being at its best, however, even in these regions, far short of the universal practice." (Vol. 6, pt. 2, p. 65). West of Alabama, commercial fertilizers were rare.

20. W. S. Thorp characterizes 1849–50 with the phrase "excellent crops except cotton" (*Business Annals* [New York: National Bureau of Economic Research, 1926], p. 125), and the Southern corn crop shows a rise over the Patent Office estimate of the previous year's production— in contrast to cotton, which shows a fall. On the corn crop for 1859–60, see the citations in Robert E. Gallman, "Self-Sufficiency in the Cotton Economy of the Antebellum South," p. 8.

mates made by the Patent Office in the 1840s.[21] If we were to regard the cotton-corn ratios of 1850 and 1860 as having equal and opposite bias, we would have the following pattern:

$$Cotton/Corn \left(\frac{000 \ bales}{000,000 \ bushels} \right)$$

	5 STATES	7 STATES	11 STATES
1840s (6 observations)	26.62	24.48	10.91
1850s (2 observations)	25.50	23.91	14.59
1870s (10 observations)	30.99	27.38	17.22
1880s (10 observations)	37.71	28.82	19.91
1890s (10 observations)	37.12	32.94	18.34

Thus, the available data suggests that in the Deep South the Civil War decade marked a watershed in terms of output proportions as well as self-sufficiency.[22]

Furthermore, the relationship between farm size and cotton-growing had changed. The census reported a drastic fall in average farm size between 1860 and 1880 (more than 60 percent in the Deep South), yet the small farms of 1880, unlike their antebellum counterparts, were heavily specialized in cotton. According to the calculations of Ransom and Sutch, the abandonment of self-sufficiency was primarily concentrated in this new, very small class of farms (largely tenants); the majority of medium and larger farms remained self-sufficient.[23]

21. The usefulness of these estimates is examined, with generally favorable conclusions, by Robert E. Gallman, "A Note on the Patent Office Crop Estimates, 1841–1848," *Journal of Economic History* 23 (June 1963), pp. 185–95. Note, however, that the corn estimates for Tennessee are especially suspect (p. 194), because the state did not come close to matching these levels until the 1890s.

22. The five states are South Carolina, Alabama, Mississippi, Louisiana, and Georgia. The seven states include Arkansas and Texas. The eleven states add North Carolina, Tennessee, Florida, and Virginia. Note, however, that the Tennessee figures render the third column suspect.

23. Ransom and Sutch, "Debt Peonage in the Cotton South After the Civil War," p. 663.

What accounts for these changes? From the late 1860s onward, many observers referred to the shift as the "overproduction of cotton," which they blamed on unwise decisions by planters, thriftlessness and carelessness on the part of tenants, and the perverse influence of merchant-creditors and the crop-lien system. Economists who have studied the postbellum South more recently have had great difficulty interpreting this argument. It is often unclear, for example, whether the critics are referring to aggregate or to microeconomic overproduction. If it is the aggregate—and the distress over falling prices in the 1870s and low prices in the 1890s suggests that the aggregate was a concern—then why should overproduction be linked to improvidence in microeconomic decisions, which had never been based on considerations of regional economic benefit? If, on the other hand, cotton is said to be overproduced at the farm level, then the economist wants to know why a lender should impose an unprofitable crop-mix on his own borrower; and even if one can find a plausible reason, how can we get around the evidence (presented in chapter 3) that cotton was in fact a more profitable crop than the alternative? [24]

These complaints have some merit. Contemporaries did not generally make the distinctions economists would like to see, and reformers surely misunderstand the nature of the incentives when they urged the farmer to "reflect that the more cotton he raises the lower the price." [25] But we must remember that the nineteenth-century Cotton South was in the historically unusual position of having a major effect on the world price of its major product, and in a period when demand was stagnant and prices falling in inverse pro-

24. These views may be found in DeCanio, pp. 111–18, 241–61; William W. Brown and Morgan O. Reynolds, "Debt Peonage Reexamined," *Journal of Economic History* 33 (December 1973); Robert Higgs, *Competition and Coercion*. Ransom and Sutch interpret "overproduction" to mean that the marginal rate of transformation of corn into cotton was below the ratio of the two prices. See Ransom and Sutch, "The 'Lock-in' Mechanism and Overproduction of Cotton in the Post-Bellum South." However, their calculation of this rate ignores the land constraint.

25. *DeBow's Review* 4 (November 1867), p. 483.

portion to the growth of output (1866–78), it is not surprising that observers were concerned. By virtue of their relationship to the world economy, Southern farmers seemed to be in a position where prudent household management coincided with the needs of the South as a region. If the elasticity of cotton demand was approximately unity (1.0), then the entire amount of the shortfall in foodstuffs was a deadweight loss to the region. If, more conservatively, the elasticity was equal to 1.5 during the transitional period 1866–79, two-thirds of the shortfall from self-sufficiency still represented a loss to the net value of regional crop production.[26]

When it came to convincing farmers that they should remain self-sufficient in their own microeconomic interest, the argument used was nothing more nor less than the safety-first argument of chapter 3. Southerners should "raise our own supplies and let cotton be surplus"; "make the plantation self-sustaining, and then what [we] can in cotton. Then a cotton crop is extra, and what it brings we can keep in our pockets." [27] When those who gave this advice used the term "diversify," they did not mean a diversified portfolio of income-earning activities, but an effort by cotton farmers "to supply most of their wants, and thereby . . . secure themselves to a large extent immunity from the evils of low prices." [28] In short, the argument was that it was imprudently risky to rely on the market for the basic subsistence needs of the farm. Throughout the transitional period 1866–79 correspondents continued to report that farmers were finally seeing the wisdom of the recommended

26. These statements assume no effect on the prices of foodstuffs. The second statement gives cotton and food crops equal weight, assuming that a 1 percent fall in food production is associated with a 1 percent rise in cotton production. Neither statement includes the cost of borrowing.

27. *DeBow's Review* 3 (April-May 1867), pp. 454, 463–64; *DeBow's Review* 4 (November 1867), pp. 483–85.

28. U.S., Congress, Senate, Committee on Agriculture and Forestry, Report 986, *Conditions of Cotton Growers* 53d Congress, 3d Session 1895, p. 43.

policy;[29] but the region never returned to its former self-sufficiency.

The problem was that the logic of self-sufficiency contains the logic of its own destruction, once a substantial deviation from the initial position occurs. The strategy of giving first priority to foodstuffs makes sense if it is possible to meet the subsistence target in this way (with reasonable confidence), and if the consequences of a shortfall are seriously costly or threatening to the family farm. However, as farm size gets smaller and smaller, eventually a point will come where the required yield per acre is too high to be met by the conservative, low-yield choice; in that case, the farmer must abandon the safety-first strategy and take on some risk in order to maximize his chances of achieving the target.[30] The need to take additional risks in order to meet high targets will be still more prevalent if farmers have acquired cash obligations, as tenants and many small farm-owners did immediately after the war. In these cases, even farmers who want to maintain self-sufficiency will find this target crowded out by the need to raise cash, if their farms are not big enough to satisfy both constraints. While the choices are fundamentally probabilistic, the essence of the matter is conveyed in the static diagram of Figure 6.1, which compares the situation of a small- and a medium-sized farmer, each of which wants to be self-sufficient in

29. See, for example, the respondents to J. R. Dodge's survey in the *Report of the Commissioner of Agriculture 1876*, pp. 148–51.

30. Formally, the problem is that there is no solution for which

$$\{ \text{probability } [mx + (1-m)y] < Z^* \} > a^*$$

hence this constraint must be abandoned, and the objective function becomes

$$\text{minimize } a' = \text{probability } [mx + (1-m)y] < Z^*.$$

In the present context, the variance of x is sufficiently greater than the variance of y that the variance of the "portfolio" is monotonically related to m. Hence the problem for these very small farms may be restated as

$$\text{probability } [y < Z^*] > a^*$$

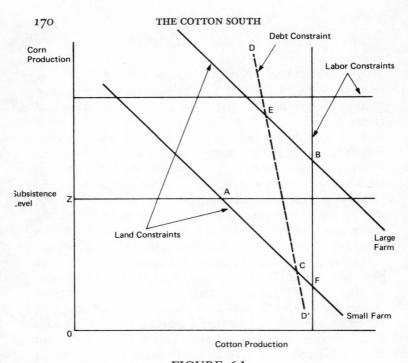

FIGURE 6.1.

The Choice of Crops with a Debt Constraint

corn at level Z, and each of which faces a debt constraint indicated by the line DD′ (the slope of which is the price of cotton divided by the price of corn). As may be seen, the larger of the two farms can produce at B (or anywhere along BE), pay its debts and enjoy a surplus of corn. The smaller farm, which would like to produce at A, must instead produce at C and buy food. It is the size of the available acreage relative to subsistence and cash needs that is crucial: the data in the top two sections of Table 6.1 show clearly that small farms pressed much more heavily against the land constraint (i.e., were farmed more intensively) than medium-scale farms and plantations.

The historical counterparts to the diagram may be quickly surveyed. The clearest case is that of the former

TABLE 6.1.
Farm Size, Factor Proportions, and Crop Mix, 1880

	SMALL FARMS	MEDIUM-SCALE FARMS	PLAN-TATIONS	ALL FARMS
Full-time laborers per 100 acres in crops				
Owned farms	9.99	5.06	3.58	8.58
Rented	12.15	5.96	....	11.00
Sharecropped	11.57		....	12.93
All types	11.22	5.35	3.31	9.52
Average expenditure on fertilizer per acre [a]				
Owned farms	$1.42	$1.00	$0.70	$1.37
Rented	1.32	0.87	....	1.21
Sharecropped	1.37		....	1.31
All types	1.50	0.95	0.76	1.33
Percentage of acreage in cotton [a]				
Owned farms	45.7	43.1	57.9	45.7
Rented	58.1	56.1	62.2	57.8
Sharecropped	53.6	50.0	74.1	53.2

SOURCES: Computed from Ransom and Sutch, "The Ex-Slave in the Post-Bellum South," pp. 141, 143, 147; Richard Sutch, personal communication to the author, May 28, 1974.

NOTE: Small farms are those reporting 50 or fewer acres in crops. Medium-scale farms are those reporting between 50 and 100 acres in crops. Plantations are those reporting 200 or more acres in crops and more than 98 weeks of hired labor, and which rely on hired labor for at least 60 percent of their requirements. The figures under "Plantations," "All types," are for all farms above 100 acres in crops.

[a] For farms reporting this variable.

slaves, for whom the failure to distribute land after the war foreclosed the option of a safety-first insulation from market uncertainties. Lacking tangible assets, the freedmen had to work for wages or borrow money in order to survive, and on the very small plots of land that black tenants farmed, self-sufficiency in foods was crowded out. The large planter, in the new situation, did not have the incentive toward food production as a form of vertical integration that he had as a slaveowner. If he paid wages, he no longer regarded his labor force as fixed for the entire year, and he no longer regarded the feeding of his workers as a fixed cost (though he may have offered wages with board in order to attract workers).[31] If he rented to tenants on shares, as most eventually did, his incentive was to keep the size of the plots small, in order to maximize the value of output per unit of land: in so doing, he made the attainment of self-sufficiency all the more difficult for the tenant. As W. L. Durst of South Carolina reported in the early 1890s:

> There is also a tendency on the part of landowners to subdivide their lands into such small farms that the tenant often does not have a sufficient quantity of land to raise both cotton and abundant food crops, and as the cotton must be grown to meet the demand for rent, supplies, fertilizers, etc., the land is mostly planted in cotton to the exclusion of food crops.[32]

The fact that tenancy implied, *ipso facto*, a commitment to make cash payments is reflected in the consistently higher concentration on cotton on tenant farms than on owned farms of comparable size (Table 6.1, third panel).

The case of the small white farmers is more complex, but not fundamentally different. In the immediate postwar period, many small farmers did not have the same access to the means of subsistence that this class had historically enjoyed, because agriculture had been disrupted by the war and swine destroyed. At the same time, the cotton price was temptingly high. So for reasons of immediate necessity and high expectations of profit, many previously independent farmers abandoned self-sufficiency. The precipitous decline in the cotton price during 1866–78 left these farmers in debt, and those debts made it extremely difficult for them to reverse their initial decision. One of the most frequent

31. The conversion of labor from a fixed to a variable factor is stressed by Robert Gallman and Ralph V. Anderson, "Slaves as Fixed Capital."
32. Senate, Report 986, p. 298.

themes in the postwar literature is the belief that the choices and events of the late 1860s had a lasting impact, forcing even the free white farmers of the South to play out the logic of a different historical path from that followed to 1860. As John Peabody of Columbus, Georgia, put it in 1883:

> I think the peculiar difficulties existing grow out of the fact that the people here were led by the high price of cotton just after the war into a craze of cotton-raising, as they call it. It was very easy to sit down with a pencil and figure out how many bales of cotton each hand would make, and what it would cost the planter to buy his corn and meat, and how many bales of cotton he would produce, and how much money he would make at 20, 25, or 30 cents a pound, and the result of this calculation was so encouraging many went into the business who knew nothing about it. They usually went into it upon borrowed money, and if it so happened that cotton declined greatly in price, or some other disaster happened to the planter, he was unable to meet his obligations. . . . So far as I know, there never has been a year when it could not be figured out satisfactorily that it was better to raise cotton and buy meat and corn, but somehow the thing did not work out that way in practice.[33]

The phrases that appear over and over in the literature of the period testify to the pressure of immediate cash requirements on crop choice: "Cotton brings money, and money pays debts"; "People in debt must raise cotton till they break"; "All that has kept them from [self-sufficiency] was trying to raise a crop that would bring money to pay their

33. U.S., Congress, Senate, Committee on Relations between Labor and Capital Report 1885, pp. 554–55. For similar interpretations, see Senate, Report 986, p. 323 and elsewhere; Hammond, pp. 121–22, 136; and the long 1889 quotation from W. J. Northen in DeCanio, pp. 108–09.

debts."[34] These observers acknowledge that cotton was usually a more profitable crop, but they assert that the Southern farmer would not have chosen cotton at the expense of self-sufficiency, unless he had to.

One of the reasons why the self-sufficiency equilibrium of 1860 proved unstable was the high cost of borrowing by small farmers, reflected in the extremely high credit prices charged for supplies by merchants (or by landlords to their tenants). These high charges are documented and highlighted by Ransom and Sutch;[35] in comparison with corn evaluated at credit prices, the claim that cotton was an unprofitable choice acquires more strength. The point made here, however, is that farmers had to borrow no matter what crops they planted, once they found themselves in the position of having inadequate supplies to get through the season. Thus, the choice of cotton was more a consequence of the need to borrow than a cause (except insofar as an initial failure in cotton had created the indebtedness). This phenomenon is well-illustrated by the plight of indebted corn-growing farmers in North Carolina, who complained that they were "forced to pay one and a half to two bushels of corn in fall for one borrowed in summer."[36] From this perspective it is to a large extent irrelevant whether the merchant-creditor or the farmer really made the decision on what crops to plant: the lender may well have insisted on a minimum acreage in cotton as security for the loan, but this requirement was only an enforcement of a decision that was inherent in the indebtedness itself.[37] Indeed, referring to Figure 6.1, the farmer who hopes to reach a state of

34. Numerous statements of this sort may be found in Senate, Report 986, pp. 288, 289, 303, 317, 327, 393.

35. Evidence on interest rates is presented in "The 'Lock-in' Mechanism," pp. 416–21. The weak state of the banking system is discussed in "Debt Peonage," pp. 643–51.

36. *First Annual Report of the Bureau of Labor Statistics of the State of North Carolina for the Year 1887* (Raleigh: J. Daniels, 1887), p. 129. See also p. 132.

37. Of course it is possible that the lender will insist on securing a *higher* probability of repayment than the farmer would provide, left to his own devices. But given the high cost of credit, one can just as plausibly argue the opposite, as the next sentence does.

self-sufficiency A at some future time may well decide to produce even more cotton (e.g., point F), in the hopes of raising funds to pay his past debts and get his family through the next growing season. But since point F is in fact a risky choice, and since the family will consume at level Z in any case, the chances of not breaking even for the year are substantially greater than they were at the unconstrained point A. The advice of the critics of overproduction was not so much to choose crops more wisely as to practice "two years of self-denial," [38] in order to get out of debt. Addressed to the poorest members of the society, this advice was just as unrealistic as Eliot Janeway telling us to put two years' income in a savings bank. In a phrase often used, small Southern farmers were "always a year behind."

This analysis is broadly supported by the figures in the third panel of Table 6.1, which show that small farms put a higher fraction of their acreage in cotton than medium-scale farms of the same tenure type, so that the size-crop mix relation now takes on a U-shape. These percentage differences do not appear large, but they correspond to very marked differences in the degree of self-sufficiency (as comparisons with the antebellum pattern will show).[39] A more general confirmation is provided by regressions using county data, explaining the fraction of acreage in cotton as a function of farm size, tenancy, and other relevant variables. For example, we obtain for 1880:

$$CS = .297 + 2.59** \frac{Ycot}{Ycrn} - .072 \frac{P}{IA} + 0.0013** \frac{IA}{F} + 0.390**T$$
$$(4.63) \qquad (1.23) \qquad (5.63)$$

$$+ 0.50**F50 - .160**F50 - 100$$
$$(2.70) \qquad (6.76)$$

$$R^2 = .401$$
$$N = 386$$

38. Charles Otken, *The Ills of the South* (New York, 1894), p. 30.
39. In Figure 6.1, as drawn, the small farm has a higher *fraction* of its acreage in cotton. But if the vertical labor-constraint were shifted to the right (i.e., if the land-labor ratio were lower on both farms), the opposite might be true. The difference in self-sufficiency would remain.

where $Ycot/Ycrn$ = ratio of yields, P/IA = county farm population per improved acre, IA/F = average farm size, T = rate of tenancy, $F50$ = percentage of farms below 50 acres, $F50 - 100$ = percentage of farms between 50 and 100 acres. The regression shows that there is still an overall positive size-cotton relationship, but that tenancy and the presence of very small farms are strongly associated with concentration in cotton.[40]

The Evolution of Tenancy

An extensive economic and historical literature deals with the nature of alternative tenancy arrangements, particularly share-tenancy, fixed-rental systems, and intermediate variations. The causes and effects of the systems have been discussed in terms of their implications for efficiency, for risk-bearing on the part of landlord and tenant, and for incentives.[41] Much of this literature seems to miss the point that as a first approximation, the patterns of farm rental simply map the distribution of assets among the farm population. This relationship is reflected in the terms of typical contracts: the lowest class of sharecroppers contributed nothing but their labor, while those who rented for cash provided a mule, implements, perhaps even seed and fertilizer. In the abstract, a fixed-rent tenancy freed the landlord of the risks of crop failure and price fall, but in practice a

40. A more extended discussion of these and related results may be found in Gavin Wright and Howard Kunreuther, "Cotton, Corn and Risk in the Nineteenth Century," pp. 542–44. The variables T and $F50$ are highly correlated, but each one appears to exert at least something of an independent effect. Very similar results are obtained for 1890.

41. Of the recent theoretical literature, see particularly J. E. Stiglitz, "Incentives and Risk Sharing in Sharecropping," *Review of Economic Studies* 41 (April 1974); Joseph D. Reid, Jr., "Sharecropping and Agricultural Uncertainty," and Reid, "Sharecropping in History and Theory," *Agricultural History* 49 (April 1975). Empirical studies of the incidence of tenure types include Robert Higgs, "Race, Tenure and Resource Allocation in Southern Agriculture, 1910," pp. 151–59, and Higgs, "Patterns of Farm Rental in the Georgia Cotton Belt, 1880–1900."

tenant without assets cannot make such a guarantee credible, neither to his landlord nor to another moneylender. The fact that landlords and merchants were willing to accept the risk inherent in a crop lein indicates the extent to which risk-distribution arrangements were limited by the asset-holdings of tenants.[42]

These constraints do not rigidly determine tenure arrangements, but they clearly placed bounds on upward mobility on this agricultural tenure ladder: a wealthy farmer might choose to operate as a tenant or sharecropper, but a poor man could not simply choose to become a cash tenant.[43] The testimony is strong that both black and white tenants hoped to move up this ladder to ultimate landownership, and one often encounters the complaint that black share tenants sought to move up to fixed-rent tenancy "prematurely" (i.e., before having the experience and ability to handle the greater risks and independent responsibility), whenever they had obtained the funds for the purchase of a mule and implements.[44] From this vantage point, the tend-

42. Nate Shaw's ability to scrape together $100 for his own mule was the key to his move from share to cash tenancy: "Got me a mule and gived up working on halves." Rosengarten, p. 118. Shaw also states that moneylenders frequently required the signature of the wife as well as the husband on notes, thus extending the loan's security to "household, kitchen plunder and all" (p. 32). Asset holdings do not, of course, explain the choice between wage labor and sharecropping at the bottom rung of the agricultural ladder.

43. The importance of this asymmetrical feature of tenancy is stressed in Clive Bell and Pinhas Zusman, "A Bargaining Theoretic Approach to Cropsharing Contracts," *American Economic Review* 66 (September 1976), esp. pp. 579–81. See also Thomas J. Edwards, "The Tenant System and Some Changes Since Emancipation," (1913), in *The Making of Black America*, edited by August Meier and Elliott Rudwick (New York: Atheneum, 1969), 2:24–26.

44. Robert Preston Brooks, *The Agrarian Revolution in Georgia, 1865–1912*, pp. 60–65. Reid stresses the efficiency advantages of sharecropping for young, inexperienced tenants, in that the system encourages continual monitoring, supervision, and assistance from the more experienced landlord. See "Sharecropping as an Understandable Market Response"; "Sharecropping and Agricultural Uncertainty," pp. 570–75; "The Theory of Share Tenancy Revisited—Again," *Journal of Political Economy* 85 (April 1977). This hypothesis will be difficult

ency of farm renters, as opposed to sharecroppers, to put a
higher fraction of their acreage into cotton is consistent with
the analysis of the previous section: because renters committed themselves to making a given payment, they had to
target a higher cash income than, *ceteris paribus*, sharecroppers. It is difficult to reconcile this fact, on the other
hand, with the view that cotton-specialization was directly
inflicted on vulnerable tenants as an exploitive instrument,
since typical sharecroppers were surely more vulnerable than
renters.

If this analysis is correct, then the trends in tenancy over
time will reflect the success of small farmers in accumulating
and retaining assets, which will in turn depend upon the
fortunes of cotton, but also on the rate of growth of the
farming population relative to cultivable land. In these basic
respects, despite the extremes of racial prejudice and dis-
crimination that existed in the South, there was an essential
sameness to the predicaments of tenants and small farmers
of both races. Elsewhere in the country, farms were growing in size and becoming more sophisticated technologically,
but in the South farms became steadily smaller under the
pressure of population, and the white tenancy rate rose
inexorably over time until, by 1900, a majority of tenants
were white. Blacks were more often in debt to their landlords, whites to country-store merchants. But both races experienced both share and fixed-rent tenancies, and it is not
clear across the South as a whole that there was any correlation between race and the mode of tenancy. In many respects, essential differences were matters of degree: blacks
had fewer opportunities outside agriculture, less legal protection against fraud and cheating, more difficulty borrowing
funds, and a harder time moving up the tenure ladder. There
is reason to believe, however, that racial constraints became
more marked and significant after 1900.

---

to distinguish from the asset-hypothesis, because age, wealth, and
experience will be correlated, and because the landlord will surely take
an active interest in the utilization of his own mule and tools by a
tenant. Many blacks, however, remained sharecroppers all their lives.

We do observe a clear inverse correlation between changes in the tenancy rate and the pace of cotton demand. It is more difficult to trace and explain changes in types of tenancy, in part because the names of tenure categories (particularly in the census) did not necessarily retain the same meaning over time. After 1900, accounts of plantation practices suggest a tightening of discipline, a loss of the early flexibility and independence of sharecropping. Increasingly, sharecropping came to be described as merely a form of piece-rate wage labor, and not a true tenancy at all.[45] The incidence of legal peonage—the literal holding of a laborer against his will—rose markedly after 1901, as did legal efforts to restrict worker mobility and competition. Such developments can be understood as a manifestation of an increasing demand for labor in the context of rising cotton demand, as well as a reflection of intensified racism and Jim Crow practices. The ease with which blacks could make the transition to cash tenancy may have declined because of these changes, even while earnings from cotton were on the increase.[46]

In this view of things, the tenancy systems of the South cannot be assigned primary blame for Southern poverty and the slow rate of progress in Southern agriculture during the nineteenth century. Alfred Marshall's classic indictment of sharecropping as an inducement to an undesirably extensive use of the soil seems highly inappropriate when applied to the small tenancies on which so much labor and fertilizer were employed. A more equitable distribution of land, a better credit system, perhaps even a different pattern of historical timing among war, emancipation, and cotton demand, might have provided more independence, more racial

45. Particularly Brooks, pp. 66–68. Brooks seems to argue that his description had *always* held, but it is very different from the descriptions of landlord-sharecropper relations of the 19th century. See also Pete Daniel, *The Shadow of Slavery.*

46. It may be that geographic as well as temporal differences explain the widely varying characterizations of sharecropping. Jay Mandle makes a case for the distinctiveness of the "plantation counties" in "The Plantation States as a Subregion of the Post-Bellum South."

and economic equity, and somewhat better terms of trade for Southern cotton over the years. Independence and equity are by no means minor aspects of human welfare, but such changes would not have produced dramatic improvements in living standards and agricultural progress. Given nineteenth-century scientific knowledge, there were sharp geographic limits on the ability of the Lower South to match the diversified, technologically advanced agriculture of the North. Southern agriculture might well have been more self-sufficient, to regional and personal benefit, but it is difficult to argue that profitable alternative commercial crops were overlooked.[47] It may well be true that the fragmentation of farms discouraged mechanization, but mechanization of cotton farming was never an answer to the problem of Southern rural poverty. When the use of tractors finally spread during the 1930s and 1940s, the immediate impact was to destroy the value of the mules and move tenants to a lower position on the tenure ladder.[48] The mechanical cotton picker ultimately reduced the numbers of poor sharecroppers and farm laborers, but only by forcing out-migration from the region.

Reprise: The Cotton South in Historical Perspective

The South was wrenched out of one historical epoch and into another during the decade of the Civil War. The dimensions of change have to do with the relations among households, wealth, and the market. Down to 1860, free Southerners were mostly independent farmers, who sharply limited the commitment of their household's labor to the market. Only under the compulsions of slavery was a high fraction

47. See particularly Julius Rubin, "The Limits of Agricultural Progress in the Nineteenth-Century South."
48. James H. Street, *The New Revolution in the Cotton Economy*, pp. 218–22; Richard H. Day, "The Economics of Technological Change and the Demise of the Sharecropper."

of a family's labor allocated to cash-crop production. The scarcity and high value of this unfree labor was a basic touchstone around which Southern economic and political life revolved. By 1880, most of the former slaves and a high percentage of the white farmers no longer had unfettered access to the means of subsistence. As Southerners well recognized, the abandonment of self-sufficiency and the rise of tenancy and indebtedness involved a basic change in the character of human relations, a surrendering of "freedom of action and industrial autonomy." Farmers now found it much more difficult to hold onto their crops waiting for a favorable price—"their obligations must be met out of the cotton as soon as it is ready for market." Small Southern farmers lost their "immunity to financial crises"; no longer could they be "relatively unscathed by the collapse of prices." And with the loss of financial independence, Southern farmers lost the right to ignore the advice and reject the supervision of others on crops and farming procedures. These changes are not, of course, so different from experiences elsewhere in history, but they represent the kind of long-run developments normally associated with the slow pressure of population against land, with basic legal, institutional, and attitudinal changes evolving over decades and centuries. In the South, it happened overnight, historically speaking.

True enough, the South had lost a bloody Civil War, but apart from the enforcement of emancipation, the changes in Southern agriculture were not imposed by a victorious North on a subjugated South. Demographic pressures did become important, but the decade of the war was associated with high mortality, a withdrawal of agricultural labor, and a decline in acreage under cultivation. The suddenness and extent of the changes in the character of Southern agriculture are explained instead by the unique historical juxtaposition of emancipation, war, and the onset of an era of stagnation in cotton demand. Land went unused, but the freedmen could not obtain it; they found themselves on small plots of land that they farmed intensively. The free farmers had their land but not their swine, and these too were pressed to meet subsistence needs through the market. Cotton was on the wane, but it appeared to be more attractive than ever.

With countless variations, two great traditions interpret and evaluate historical trends in the relationship between households and markets: the tradition of most economists, descended from Adam Smith, which views the spread of markets and specialized production as a progressive development, an improvement of resource allocation, an encouragement to advancements in knowledge and progress, and an opportunity for higher standards of living on and off the farm; and the tradition of Marxian writers (though in this American application with a strong Jeffersonian flavor as well), which views the market as an invading, intruding force, a maelstrom that lures or sucks households into its orbit, whirling them in historical circles beyond their control, and permitting no escape. Usually these traditions talk past each other, obscuring the extent to which each one contains elements of truth in describing the same historical developments, and failing to ask why it is that some cases fit one version, some the other. The suddenness of change in the nineteenth-century Cotton South, and the absence of significant technological progress or economies of scale, illustrate several points of broader historical relevance.

Although specialized production for the market is more profitable and more efficient as resource allocation, it does not necessarily follow that individuals will freely choose to specialize at the expense of self-sufficiency in basic commodities of subsistence. An involuntary movement into specialized production can occur, however, without the use of state or judicial power. Undoubtedly, the planters knew what they were doing in opposing the redistribution of their own land to the freedmen; but to a great extent, the pressures of indebtedness and the exigencies of the time played the same role as the imposition of taxes in European state-building efforts or in African labor-supply-generating policies, without a collective class or state interest in this result. Southern farmers moved heavily into production for the market at a time of general apprehension about the overproduction of cotton, reflecting the correct perception that the region would have been better off growing less cotton, not more.

More generally, the case also shows that increasing specialization, division of labor, and exchange—all of which enhanced economic efficiency in conventional terms—had no necessary connection with the emergence of a prosperous, progressive agriculture, the improvement of living standards, or the acceleration of technological progress. This is so, not just because the South was in a position to depress the world's cotton price by expanding production, but because the choice of cash crops was limited, demand for cotton was slow, and the region's manufacturing sector was late developing. The opposite conditions held true in the North, and hence it made sense for that region's farmers to welcome the market with open arms. They too, however, made similar complaints when demand fell off in the 1890s and again after World War I. Moralists can view these agrarian protests as after-the-fact scapegoating by farmers who chose to gamble and lost, though this is certainly not the only possible interpretation. In the South it is truer to say that the choices were thrust upon farmers by larger events and forces. The malaise of the postbellum South, the disputes and anxiety over tenancies, crop liens, interest charges, and overproduction, all confirm the rationality of the antebellum farmers who grew cotton only as a surplus crop. The behavior of these free households explains the demand for slave labor and the flourishing success of slavery during the era when cotton was king. Postwar circumstances and institutions pushed farmers of both races toward the alternative rationality of the market, but the forces of market demand after 1860 were too weak to restore economic progress based on cotton. As demographic pressures developed and the fragmentation of farms continued, the constraints on Southern farmers intensified over time. Thus, not just slavery, but the self-sufficient prosperity of 1860, was gone with the wind forever. The only escape came with the massive departure of Southerners from agriculture. In this era of enthusiasm for the New South of the twentieth century, one might almost forget that the problems of Southern agricultural development were never really solved.

Bibliography

The following is a selected list of the secondary works used in this study.

* = available in paperback edition.

* Aitken, Hugh, ed. *Did Slavery Pay?* Boston: Houghton Mifflin, 1971.

Anderson, Ralph V. "Labor Utilization and Productivity, Diversification and Self-Sufficiency, Southern Plantations, 1800–1840." Doctoral dissertation, University of North Carolina, 1974.

Atherton, Lewis E. *The Southern County Store 1800–1860.* Baton Rouge: Louisiana State University Press, 1949.

Aufhauser, Keith. "Slavery and Scientific Management," *Journal of Economic History* 33 (December 1973).

Banks, Enoch Marvin. *The Economics of Land Tenure in Georgia.* New York: Columbia University Press, 1905.

Barney, William L. *The Secessionist Impulse: Alabama and Mississippi in 1860.* Princeton: Princeton University Press, 1974.

Bateman, Fred, and Thomas Weiss. "Comparative Regional Development in Antebellum Manufacturing," *Journal of Economic History* 35 (March 1975).

Bateman, Fred, James Foust, and Thomas Weiss. "Profitability in Southern Manufacturing: Estimates for 1860," *Explorations in Economic History* 12 (July 1975).

Battalio, Raymond C., and John Kagel. "The Structure of Antebellum Southern Agriculture: South Carolina, A Case Study," *Agricultural History* 44 (January 1970).

Benson, Lee. "Explanations of American Civil War Causation." In *Toward the Scientific Study of History.* Philadelphia: J. B. Lippincott, 1972.

Bernstein, Barton J. "Southern Politics and Attempts to Reopen the African Slave Trade," *Journal of Negro History* 51 (January 1966).

* Berwanger, Eugene. *The Frontier Against Slavery*. Urbana, Illinois: University of Illinois Press, 1967.
* Blassingame, John. *The Slave Community*. New York: Oxford University Press, 1972.
Bogue, Allan G. *From Prairie to Corn Belt*. Chicago: University of Chicago Press, 1963.
Bonner, James C. "Profile of a Late Antebellum Community." *American Historical Review* 49 (July 1944).
Bonner, James C. *A History of Georgia Agriculture 1732–1860*. Atlanta: Georgia University Press, 1964.
Brady, Eugene A. "A Reconsideration of the Lancashire 'Cotton Famine.'" *Agricultural History* 37 (July 1963).
Brooks, Robert Preston. *The Agrarian Revolution in Georgia, 1865–1912*. Madison: Bulletin of the University of Wisconsin, 1914.
Brown, Harry Bates. *Cotton*. New York: McGraw-Hill, 1927.
* Cairnes, John E. *The Slave Power*. New York: Harper Torchbook, 1969. First published 1862.
Campbell, Randolph. "Planters and Plain Folk: Harrison County, Texas, as a Test Case, 1850–1860." *Journal of Southern History* 40 (August 1974).
* Channing, Steven. *Crisis of Fear*. New York: W. W. Norton & Co., 1974. First published 1970.
Clark, Blanche Henry. *The Tennessee Yeoman, 1840–1860*. Nashville: Vanderbilt University Press, 1942.
Conrad, Alfred H. and Meyer, John R. "The Economics of Slavery in the Antebellum South," *Journal of Political Economy* 66 (April 1958). Reprinted in Aitken, *op. cit.*
Cooper, William J. "The Cotton Crisis in the Antebellum South: Another Look," *Agricultural History* 49 (April 1975).
Covert, James R. "Seedtime and Harvest." U.S. Department of Agriculture, Bureau of Statistics Bulletin 85 (1912).
* Craven, Avery. *An Historian and the Civil War*. Chicago: University of Chicago Press, 1964.
Danhof, Clarence. *Change in Agriculture: The Northern United States 1820–1870*. Cambridge: Harvard University Press, 1969.
* Daniel, Pete. *The Shadow of Slavery: Peonage in the South 1901–1969*. Urbana: University of Illinois Press, 1972.
* David, Paul A., Herbert G. Gutman, Richard Sutch, Peter Temin, and Gavin Wright. *Reckoning With Slavery*. New York: Oxford University Press, 1976.
David, Paul A. "The Mechanization of Reaping in the Ante-

Bellum Midwest." In *Industrialization in Two Systems*, edited by Henry Rosovsky. New York: John Wiley & Sons, 1966.

Davis, Charles S. *The Cotton Kingdom in Alabama*. Montgomery: Alabama State Department of Archives and History, 1939.

* Davis, David B. *The Problem of Slavery in Western Culture*. Ithaca: Cornell University Press, 1966.

Davis, David B. *The Slave Power Conspiracy and the Paranoid Style*. Ithaca: Cornell University Press, 1966.

Day, Richard H. "The Economics of Technological Change and the Demise of the Sharecropper," *American Economic Review* 57 (June 1967).

DeCanio, Stephen. *Agriculture in the Postbellum South*. Cambridge: M.I.T. Press, 1974.

Decker, Leslie E. "The Great Speculation: An Interpretation of Mid-Continent Pioneering." In *The Frontier in American Development*, edited by David M. Ellis. Ithaca: Cornell University Press, 1969.

Denman, Clarence Phillips. *The Secession Movement in Alabama*. Montgomery: Alabama State Department of Archives and History, 1933.

Domar, Evsey. "The Causes of Slavery or Serfdom: A Hypothesis," *Journal of Economic History* 30 (March 1970).

Donnell, Ezekiel J. *Chronological and Statistical History of Cotton*. New York, 1872.

Dumond, Dwight L., ed. *Southern Editorials on Secession*. Gloucester, Mass.: Peter Smith, 1964. First published 1931.

Dyer, Gustavus. *Democracy in the South Before the Civil War*. New York: Arno Press, 1973. First published 1905.

Easterlin, Richard. "Population Change and Farm Settlement in the Northern United States," *Journal of Economic History* 36 (March 1976).

Easterlin, Richard. "Farm Production and Income in Old and New Areas at Mid-Century." In *Essays in Nineteenth Century Economic History*, edited by David C. Klingaman and Richard K. Vedder. Athens: Ohio University Press, 1975.

Elkins, Stanley, and Eric McKitrick. "A Meaning for Turner's Frontier," *Political Science Quarterly* 69 (September-December 1954).

Emerson, F. V. "Geographic Influences in American Slavery," *Bulletin of the American Geographic Society* 43 (January-March 1911).

Engerman, Stanley. "Some Considerations Relating to Property Rights in Man," *Journal of Economic History* 33 (March 1973).

Engerman, Stanley. "A Reconsideration of Southern Economic Growth, 1770–1860," *Agricultural History* 49 (April 1975).

Farley, Reynolds. "The Urbanization of Negroes in the United States," *Journal of Social History* 1 (Spring 1968).

Field, Alexander. "Educational Reform and Manufacturing Development in Mid-Nineteenth Century Massachusetts." Doctoral dissertation, University of California at Berkeley, 1974.

Fischbaum, Marvin, and Julius Rubin. "Slavery and the Economic Development of the South," *Explorations in Economic History* 6 (Fall 1968).

* Fitzhugh, George. *Cannibals All! Or, Slaves Without Masters.* Cambridge, Mass.: The Belknap Press, 1960. First published 1857.

Fleisig, Heywood. "Slavery, the Supply of Agricultural Labor, and the Industrialization of the South," *Journal of Economic History* 36 (September 1976).

* Fogel, Robert W., and Stanley L. Engerman. *Time on the Cross: The Economics of American Negro Slavery.* Two volumes. Boston: Little-Brown, 1974.

Fogel, Robert W., and Stanley L. Engerman. "The Economics of Slavery," in *The Reinterpretation of American Economic History*, edited by Fogel and Engerman. New York: Harper & Row, 1971.

Fogel, Robert W., and Stanley L. Engerman. "Explaining the Relative Efficiency of Slave Agriculture in the Antebellum South," *American Economic Review* 67 (June 1977).

Foner, Eric. "The Causes of the Civil War: Recent Interpretations and New Directions," *Civil War History* 20 (September 1970).

Foner, Philip S. *Business and Slavery.* Chapel Hill: University of North Carolina Press, 1941.

Foust, James D., and Dale E. Swan. "Productivity and Profitability of Antebellum Slave Labor: A Micro Approach," *Agricultural History* 44 (January 1970).

Foust, James D. "The Yeoman Farmer and Westward Expansion of U.S. Cotton Production," Doctoral dissertation, University of North Carolina, 1967. Reprinted by Arno Press, 1976.

* Freehling, William W. *Prelude to Civil War.* New York: Harper and Row, 1966.

Freehling, William W. "The Founding Fathers and Slavery," *American Historical Review* 77 (February 1972).

Gallman, Robert E. "Trends in the Size Distribution of Wealth in the Nineteenth Century: Some Speculations." In Conference on Research in Income and Wealth, *Six Papers on the Size Distribution of Wealth and Income*. Studies in Income and Wealth, Volume 33. New York: Columbia University Press, 1969.

Gallman, Robert E. "Self-Sufficiency in the Cotton Economy of the Antebellum South," *Agricultural History* 44 (January 1970).

Gallman, Robert E. "The Agricultural Sector and the Pace of Economic Growth." In *Essays in Nineteenth Century Economic History*, edited by David C. Klingaman and Richard K. Vedder. Athens: Ohio University Press, 1975.

Gallman, Robert E., and Ralph V. Anderson. "Slaves as Fixed Capital," *Journal of American History* 64 (June 1977).

Gates, Paul W. *The Farmer's Age: Agriculture 1815–1860*. New York: Holt, Rinehart and Winston, 1960.

* Genovese, Eugene. *The Political Economy of Slavery*. New York: Pantheon, 1965.

Genovese, Eugene. *The World the Slaveholders Made*. New York: Pantheon, 1969.

Genovese, Eugene. "Yeoman Farmers in a Slaveholders' Democracy," *Agricultural History* 49 (April 1975).

* Genovese, Eugene. *Roll, Jordan, Roll*. New York: Pantheon, 1974.

Goldin, Claudia. *Urban Slavery in the South 1820–1860*. Chicago: University of Chicago Press, 1976.

Gray, Lewis Cecil. *History of Agriculture in the Southern United States to 1860*. Two volumes. Washington: Carnegie Institution, 1933.

Green, Fletcher M. "Democracy in the Old South," *Journal of Southern History* 12 (February 1946).

* Gutman, Herbert G. *The Black Family in Slavery and Freedom 1750–1925*. New York: Pantheon, 1976.

Hammond, Matthew B. *The Cotton Industry*. New York: MacMillan, 1897.

Hendrix, James Paisley, Jr. "The Efforts to Reopen the African Slave Trade in Louisiana," *Louisiana History* 10 (Spring 1969).

Higgs, Robert. "Race, Tenure and Resource Allocation in Southern Agriculture, 1910," *Journal of Economic History* 33 (March 1973).

Higgs, Robert. "Patterns of Farm Rental in the Georgia Cotton Belt, 1880–1900," *Journal of Economic History* 34 (June 1974).

Higgs, Robert. *Competition and Coercion.* New York: Cambridge University Press, 1977.

Hilliard, Sam Bowers. *Hog Meat and Hoe Cake: Food Supply in the Old South, 1840–1860.* Carbondale: Southern Illinois University Press, 1972.

Kelly, John. "The End of the Famine: The Manchester Cotton Trade, 1864–67." In *Textile History and Economic History,* edited by N. B. Harte and K. P. Ponting. Manchester: Manchester University Press, 1973.

* Knoles, George Harmon (ed.) *The Crisis of the Union.* Baton Rouge: Louisiana State University Press, 1965.

Kolchin, Peter, *First Freedom.* Westport, Conn.: Greenwood Press, 1972.

Kotlikoff, Laurence, and Sebastian E. Pinera. "The Old South's Stake in the Inter-Regional Movement of Slaves, 1850–1860," *Journal of Economic History* 37 (June 1977).

Linden, Fabian. "Economic Democracy in the Slave South: An Appraisal of Some Recent Views," *Journal of Negro History* 31 (April 1946).

* Lynd, Staughton. "On Turner, Beard and Slavery," *Journal of Negro History* 48 (1963). Reprinted in Lynd's *Class Conflict, Slavery, and the United States Constitution.* Indianapolis: Bobbs-Merrill, 1967.

Mandle, Jay. "The Plantation States as a Subregion of the Post-Bellum South," *Journal of Economic History* 34 (September 1974).

Mayhew, Anne. "A Reappraisal of the Causes of Farm Protest in the United States, 1870–1900," *Journal of Economic History* 32 (June 1972).

McCay, C. F. "Cultivation of Cotton." In *Eighty Years' Progress of the United States.* New York, 1864.

McDonald, Forrest, and Grady McWhiney. "The Antebellum Southern Herdsman: A Reinterpretation," *Journal of Southern History* 41 (May 1975).

McGuire, Robert, and Robert Higgs. "Cotton, Corn and Risk: Another View," *Explorations in Economic History* 14 (April 1977).

Mellman, Robert. "A Reinterpretation of the Economic History of the Post-Reconstruction South, 1877–1919." Doctoral dissertation, Massachusetts Institute of Technology, 1975.

Metzer, Jacob. "Rational Management, Modern Business Practices, and Economies of Scale in the Ante-Bellum Southern Plantations," *Explorations in Economic History* 12 (April 1975).

Miller, William L. "Slavery and the Population of the South," *Southern Economic Journal* 28 (July 1961).

Moore, John H. *Agriculture in Ante-Bellum Mississippi.* New York: Bookman Associates, 1958.

* Moore, Barrington. "The American Civil War: The Last Capitalist Revolution." In *Social Origins of Dictatorship and Democracy.* Boston: Beacon Press, 1966.

* Morgan, Edmund S. *American Slavery, American Freedom.* New York: W. W. Norton & Company, 1975.

* North, Douglass. *The Economic Growth of the United States, 1790–1860.* New York: W. W. Norton & Company, 1966. First published 1961.

O'Connor, Thomas H. *Lords of the Loom: The Cotton Whigs and the Coming of the Civil War.* New York: Charles Scribner's Sons, 1968.

Olsen, Otto. "Historians and the Extent of Slave Ownership in the Southern United States," *Civil War History* 18 (June 1972).

Owens, Leslie Howard. *This Species of Property.* New York: Oxford University Press, 1976.

Owsley, Frank. *Plain Folk of the Old South.* Baton Rouge: Louisiana State University Press, 1949.

Parker, William N. "The Slave Plantation in American Agriculture." In *Essays in American Economic History*, edited by A. W. Coats and R. M. Robertson. London: Edward Arnold, 1969.

Parker, William N. "Slavery and Southern Economic Development," *Agricultural History* 44 (January 1970).

Parker, William N. (ed.) *The Structure of the Cotton Economy of the Antebellum South.* Originally the January, 1970, issue of *Agricultural History.* Berkeley: University of California Press, 1970.

Parker, William N. "Agriculture." In Lance Davis, Richard Easterlin, William N. Parker *et al, American Economic Growth.* New York: Harper & Row, 1972.

Parker, William N. "The Social Bases of Regional History." In *Essays in Nineteenth Century Economic History,* edited by David C. Klingaman and Richard K. Vedder. Athens: Ohio University Press, 1975.

Passell, Peter, and Gavin Wright. "The Effects of Pre-Civil War Territorial Expansion on the Price of Slaves," *Journal of Political Economy* 80 (November/December 1972).

Passell, Peter, and Maria Schmundt. "Pre-Civil War Land Policy and the Growth of Manufacturing," *Explorations in Economic History* 9 (Fall 1971).

Phifer, Edward. "Slavery in Microcosm: Burke County, North Carolina," *Journal of Southern History* 28 (1962).

* Phillips, Ulrich B. "The Economic Cost of Slaveholding in the Cotton Belt," *Political Science Quarterly* 20 (June 1905). Reprinted in *Ulrich B. Phillips: The Slave Economy of the Old South,* edited by Eugene Genovese. Baton Rouge: Louisiana State University Press, 1968.

Phillips, Ulrich B. "The Origin and Growth of the Southern Black Belts," *American Historical Review* 11 (July 1906).

* Phillips, Ulrich B. *American Negro Slavery.* New York: D. Appleton and Company, 1918.

* Phillips, Ulrich B. *Life and Labor in the Old South.* Boston: Little, Brown, 1963. First published 1929.

* Potter, David. *The Impending Crisis 1848–1861.* New York: Harper and Row, 1976.

Prunty, Merle. "The Renaissance of the Southern Plantation," *The Geographical Review* 45 (October 1955).

Rainwater, Percy L. "Economic Benefits of Secession: Opinions in Mississippi in the 1850s," *Journal of Southern History* 1 (November 1935).

Rainwater, Percy L. *Mississippi, Storm Center of Secession 1856–1861.* Baton Rouge: Otto Claitor, 1938.

Ramsdell, Charles W. "The Natural Limits of Slavery Expansion," *Mississippi Valley Historical Review* 16 (September 1929).

Ransom, Roger, and Richard Sutch. "Debt Peonage in the Cotton South After the Civil War," *Journal of Economic History* 32 (September 1972).

Ransom, Roger, and Richard Sutch. "The Ex-Slave in the Post-Bellum South," *Journal of Economic History* 33 (March 1973).

Ransom, Roger, and Richard Sutch. "The Impact of the Civil

War and of Emancipation on Southern Agriculture," *Explorations in Economic History* 12 (January 1975).

Ransom, Roger, and Richard Sutch. "The 'Lock-in' Mechanism and Overproduction of Cotton in the Post-Bellum South," *Agricultural History* 49 (April 1975).

* Ransom, Roger, and Richard Sutch. *One Kind of Freedom.* New York: Cambridge University Press, 1977.

Reid, Joseph D., Jr. "Sharecropping as an Understandable Market Response," *Journal of Economic History* 33 (March 1973).

Reid, Joseph D., Jr. "Sharecropping and Agricultural Uncertainty," *Economic Development and Cultural Change* 24 (April 1976).

Rosengarten, Theodore. *All God's Dangers: The Life of Nate Shaw.* New York: Alfred A. Knopf, 1975.

Rothstein, Morton. "The Big Farm: Abundance and Scale in American Agriculture," *Agricultural History* 49 (October 1975).

Rubin, Julius. "Urban Growth and Regional Development." In *The Growth of Seaport Cities 1790–1825*, edited by David T. Gilchrist. Charlottesville: University of Virginia Press, 1967.

Rubin, Julius. "The Limits of Agricultural Progress in the Nineteenth-Century South," *Agricultural History* 49 (April 1975).

Russel, Robert R. *Economic Aspects of Southern Sectionalism.* New York: Russell & Russell, 1960. First published 1924.

Russel, Robert R. "The General Effects of Slavery Upon Southern Economic Progress," *Journal of Southern History* 4 (February 1938).

Russel, Robert R. "The Effects of Slavery Upon Nonslaveholders in the Ante-Bellum South," *Agricultural History* 15 (April 1941).

Sandberg, Lars. *Lancashire in Decline.* Columbus: Ohio State University Press, 1974.

Sellers, Charles G. "The Travail of Slavery." In *The Southerner as American.* Chapel Hill: University of North Carolina Press, 1960.

* Shugg, Roger W. *Origins of Class Struggle in Louisiana.* Baton Rouge: Louisiana State University Press, 1939.

Soltow, Lee. "Economic Inequality in the United States in the Period from 1790 to 1860," *Journal of Economic History* 31 (December 1971).

Soltow, Lee. *Men and Wealth in the United States 1850–1870.* New Haven: Yale University Press, 1975.

* Stampp, Kenneth M. *The Peculiar Institution: Slavery in the Ante-Bellum South.* New York: Alfred A. Knopf, 1956.

* Stampp, Kenneth M. *The Causes of the Civil War.* Englewood Cliffs, N.J.: Prentice-Hall, 1965.

* Starobin, Robert S. *Industrial Slavery in the Old South.* New York: Oxford University Press, 1970.

Street, James H. *The New Revolution in the Cotton Economy.* Chapel Hill: University of North Carolina Press, 1957.

Takaki, Ronald. *A Pro-Slavery Crusade.* New York: The Free Press, 1971.

Temin, Peter. "The Causes of Cotton-Price Fluctuations in the 1830's," *Review of Economics and Statistics* 49 (November 1967).

Temin, Peter. "The Post-Bellum Recovery of the South and the Cost of the Civil War," *Journal of Economic History* 36 (December 1976).

Thornton, J. Mills. "Politics and Power in a Slave Society: Alabama 1806–1860." Unpublished Ph.D. dissertation, Yale University, 1974.

Todd, J. A. *The World's Cotton Crops.* New York, 1912.

United States Bureau of the Census. *Historical Statistics of the United States, Colonial Times to 1957.* Washington: Government Printing Office, 1960.

United States Office of Agricultural Experiment Stations. *The Cotton Plant.* Bulletin Number 33. Washington: G.P.O., 1896.

* Wade, Richard C. *Slavery in the Cities.* New York: Oxford University Press, 1964.

Wallerstein, Immanuel. "American Slavery and the Capitalist World-Economy," *American Journal of Sociology* 81 (March 1976).

Watkins, James L. *King Cotton.* New York, 1908.

Weaver, Herbert. *Mississippi Farmers, 1850–1860.* Nashville: Vanderbilt University Press, 1945.

Weiher, Kenneth. "The Cotton Industry and Southern Urbanization," *Explorations in Economic History* 14 (April 1977).

* Wharton, Vernon. *The Negro in Mississippi 1865–1890.* New York: Harper Torchbook, 1965. First published 1947.

Wiener, Jonathan M. "Planter-Merchant Conflict in Reconstruction Alabama," *Past and Present* 68 (August 1975).

Wish, Harvey. "The Revival of the African Slave Trade in the United States 1856–1860," *Mississippi Valley Historical Review* 27 (March 1941).

Wolff, Gerald. "The Slavocracy and the Homestead Problem of 1854,"*Agricultural History* 40 (April 1966).

Wooster, Ralph A. *The Secession Conventions of the South.* Princeton: Princeton University Press, 1962.

Wooster, Ralph A. *The People in Power: Courthouse and Statehouse in the Lower South, 1850–1860.* Knoxville: The University of Tennessee Press, 1969.

Wright, Gavin. " 'Economic Democracy' and the Concentration of Agricultural Wealth in the Cotton South, 1850–1860," *Agricultural History* 44 (January 1970).

Wright, Gavin. "An Econometric Study of Cotton Production and Trade, 1830–1860," *Review of Economics and Statistics* 53 (May 1971).

Wright, Gavin. "Cotton Competition and the Post-Bellum Recovery of the American South," *Journal of Economic History* 34 (September 1974).

Wright, Gavin, and Howard Kunreuther. "Cotton, Corn and Risk in the Nineteenth Century," *Journal of Economic History* 35 (September 1975).

* Wright, Gavin. "Prosperity, Progress and American Slavery." In Paul David *et al, Reckoning With Slavery, op. cit.*

Wright, Gavin, and Howard Kunreuther. "Cotton, Corn and Risk in the Nineteenth Century: A Reply," *Explorations in Economic History* 14 (April 1977).

Yarwood, Dean. "Legislative Persistence: A Comparison of the U.S. Senate in 1850 and 1860," *Midwest Journal of Political Science* 11 (May 1967).

Yarwood, Dean. "A Failure in Coalition Maintenance: The Defection of the South Prior to the Civil War." In *The Study of Coalition Behavior,* edited by S. Groennings. New York: Holt, Rinehart & Winston, 1970.

Yasuba, Yasukichi. "The Profitability and Viability of Plantation Slavery in the United States," *Economic Studies Quarterly* 12 (September 1961). Reprinted in Aitken (ed.), *op. cit.*

* Zilversmit, Arthur. *The First Emancipation.* Chicago: University of Chicago Press, 1967.

Index